# ASTRO~NAVIGATION BY CALCULATOR

## A Handbook for Yachtsmen

### Henry Levison

DAVID & CHARLES
Newton Abbot   London   North Pomfret (Vt)

**British Library Cataloguing in Publication Data**

Levison, Henry
   Astro-navigation by calculator.
   1. Nautical astronomy—Data processing
   2. Calculating-machines
   I. Title
   623.89      VK560

   ISBN 0-7153-8553-4

First published 1984
Second impression 1987

© Henry Levison 1984, 1987

Typeset by ABM Typographics Limited, Hull
and printed in Great Britain
by A. Wheaton & Co, Hennock Road, Exeter
for David & Charles (Publishers) Limited
Brunel House   Newton Abbot   Devon

Published in the United States of America
by David & Charles Inc
North Pomfret   Vermont 05053   USA

# Contents

# Acknowledgements

This book could not have been written without the formulae and tables introduced by Dr B. D. Yallop in the Royal Greenwich Observatory Bulletin No. 185, 'Compact Data for Navigation and Astronomy for 1981 to 1985'. Extracts from these tables are reproduced with permission, from data supplied by the Science and Engineering Research Council.

I am also indebted to: Mr E. Rattner BSc for enlightening me on the potential of calculators for navigation, and providing advice on all matters mathematical; Dr P. R. Levison for the illustrations; Capt J. C. Craigie for such helpful and constructive comments on the manuscript; and my wife for her forbearance throughout the preparation of this book.

# Abbreviations

| | | | |
|---|---|---|---|
| Az | azimuth | Hs | sextant altitude |
| D | dip | IE | index error |
| d | great circle distance | Lat | latitude |
| Dec | declination | LHA | local hour angle |
| dep | departure | LHAγ | local hour angle Aries |
| d.Lat | difference in latitude | LHA* | local hour angle star |
| d.Long | difference in longitude | LL | lower limb |
| DMP | difference of meridional parts | Long | longitude |
| | | Longh | longitude in hours |
| EP | estimated position | LT | local time |
| GD | Greenwich date | M Pts | meridional parts |
| GHA | Greenwich hour angle | p | i) intercept ii) polar distance |
| GHAγ | Greenwich hour angle Aries | P→R | conversion of polar to rectangular co-ordinates |
| GHA* | Greenwich hour angle star | | |
| GMT | Greenwich mean time | R | refraction |
| GP | geographical position | R→P | conversion of rectangular to polar co-ordinates |
| H | apparent altitude | | |
| h | height of eye (m) | S | semi-diameter |
| Hc | calculated altitude | SHA | sidereal hour angle |
| Ho | true observed altitude | UL | upper limb |
| HP | horizontal parallax | ZT | zone time |

4

# Introduction

Professional seamen attain proficiency in astro-navigation by virtue of long training and constant practice. Most yachtsmen do not have this opportunity and obtain their grasp of the subject by attending relatively short evening courses or teaching themselves. Many give up; perhaps deterred by the lengthy procedure of consulting books of astronomical tables, completing a long series of simple sums and then plotting a position. Fortunately the whole process has now been greatly simplified and shortened by the irresistible advance of pocket calculators and the introduction of special calculator tables.

The purpose of this book is to show yachtsmen an alternative approach to astro-navigation, by dispensing with nautical almanacs, sight reduction tables, plotting sheets, graph paper, time and date problems, and all the complications associated with traditional methods. The microchip has come to stay and there is no point in masochistically adhering to traditional methods when one can get more accurate results in a much shorter time with an inexpensive scientific calculator and a digital watch. This book will demonstrate how the whole process of obtaining a fix from sextant sights can be achieved entirely by pocket calculator, without drawing a single line on a chart, plotting sheet or graph paper, or using any of the traditional tables.

An obvious disadvantage of relying on a calculator is the possibility of the calculator failing, but this is unlikely if it is treated with care and spare batteries are carried. In fact, calculators are cheap enough to carry a spare one anyway. The fact remains, however, that a calculator could fail with no spares available. Traditional methods must then be used and, for this reason, they should be known and the appropriate tables kept on board. But, all being well, there should be no need to use them except as an occasional exercise to check calculator workings. Such exercises are strongly recommended, however, as they have a threefold value: giving calculator users confidence in their results; revealing blunders caused by incorrect key strokes; and, conversely, as a check on traditional methods themselves.

Yachtsmen who have not learned traditional methods will find them easier to understand and apply after using this book; whilst those who already practise traditional methods will get quicker and more accurate results with a calculator. Some may decide to combine both methods by using a nautical almanac for some parts of the process and a calculator for others. But all should realise that a calculator cannot do anything that cannot be done by traditional methods. It is just an easier and quicker way of achieving the same end result. Those who wish to compare the two methods are advised to read *Navigation for Offshore and Ocean Sailors* by David Derrick (David & Charles, 1981) for the traditional approach.

Each chapter includes worked examples and concludes with a summary of calculator formulae and an exercise for practice, with the answers and required tables at the end of the book. Answers are given in step-by-step detail, allowing each stage of a calculation to be checked and errors traced; this approach should be followed in practice. All the examples and exercises have been done with a simple non-programmable calculator, although it is easier and quicker to use a programmable model. Calculator programmes have not been included as there are so many different calculators on the market, with differing capacities, that it would not be practicable to give programmes, or to update them as new models are introduced. However, it is a simple matter to write your own programmes by following the manufacturer's instructions and using the formulae in this book.

# 1

# Equipment

Basic equipment for astro-navigation consists of a sextant, digital watch, scientific calculator and astronomical tables.

A sextant is used to measure the altitudes of observed heavenly bodies. A digital watch is required for the *exact* time and date of each sextant sight. A position could then be fixed by traditional methods using nautical almanacs and sight reduction tables, and plotting position lines on a chart, plotting sheet or graph paper. In this book we shall not be using such laborious methods; we shall fix our position rapidly, simply and directly by pocket calculator from a very special book of astronomical tables.

## Sextants

Taking a sextant sight from a yacht in rough seas, just a few feet above sea level, is far more difficult than from the bridge of a super-tanker. A yachtsman's sextant must be robust enough to withstand accidental bumps and constructed of materials which are resistant to seawater corrosion; yet inexpensive enough to replace if damaged or lost overboard. The latter event terminates any further position fixing by astro-navigation, so it is safer for yachtsmen to possess two cheap plastic sextants rather than one expensive instrument. However, you get what you pay for and there is no doubt that an expensive sextant will be superior to an inexpensive one; but for practical purposes an inexpensive plastic sextant can suffice for ocean navigation.

## Navigator's Watch

Astro-navigation is based upon sextant sights but the ensuing calculations depend on knowing the exact time, correct to the nearest second, at which the sight was taken. The science of astro-navigation preceded, and was responsible for, the development of ships' chronometers. These are expensive and not designed for use in small yachts but, fortunately for us, the microchip has again revolutionised this aspect of navigation. Cheap waterproof digital watches are now available which are far better for navigational purposes than the most expensive clockwork ships' chronometer.

The required features of a yacht navigator's watch are:

1 Accuracy.
2 Continuous digital display of hours, minutes and seconds in 24 hour mode.
3 Display of date.
4 Waterproof.
5 Easy setting to correct time.
6 Prolonged battery life.

All these features, and others, are included in the Casio W 100 watch costing less than £20. It is accurate and displays hours, minutes, seconds, day and date; and automatically keeps the correct date irrespective of the number of days in the month or year. But its most useful feature is ease of setting to correct time. Just before a radio time signal is due, the minutes are adjusted to zero (if necessary). By pressing a button at the time signal, the seconds automatically reset to zero. As the watch is accurate to less than a second a day, it need only be checked once daily by radio time signal and reset if necessary.

Other useful, but not essential, features of this watch include: an alarm (for remembering to switch on the radio); an hourly bleep signal (for remembering to read the log or barometer); a stop watch (for timing light signals); illumination of the dial and a five-year battery life.

These features allow us to cast away former problems of converting zone time and date to Greenwich time as the watch maintains accurate Greenwich time and date in the 24-hour mode.

**Pocket Calculator**

By using a simple inexpensive scientific calculator, all the arithmetic can be eliminated from astro-navigation. The calculator must have the following essential functions:

1 Keys for sin, cos, tan, $x^2$, $1/x$, $\sqrt{x}$, and parentheses. All these are used for the basic calculations.
2 A key for converting polar to rectangular co-ordinates. It may be designated PR, P→R or rθ, according to the model, and is used for finding the estimated position.
3 A key for converting minutes and seconds into decimals of a degree or hour. This simplifies and hastens all the calculations.
4 At least three memories. This again simplifies and hastens calculations and saves writing down intermediate results.

Desirable but inessential features are:

1 Liquid crystal display for prolonged battery life.
2 Constant memory. This retains data in memory even when switched off.
3 Automatic power cut-off. This prevents battery drain if you forget to switch off the calculator.

Programmable calculators are best, and the more programme steps and memories they have the quicker they will produce the answers. However, a non-programmable calculator will fulfil all requirements provided it has the essential functions mentioned. The only difference is that it requires more key strokes and takes longer, but it still produces exactly the same answer.

Suitable non-programmable calculators are much cheaper than programmables but are becoming scarcer as more and more cheap programmables come on to the market. At the time of writing, one of the cheapest suitable calculators which is generally available is the programmable Casio 180P, with seven memories. The most expensive calculators are very advanced and versatile instruments which are better described as pocket computers, eg Texas TI66, Casio 602P, Sharp PC1211, Hewlett-Packard 41CV. Some have alphanumeric keyboards and can be programmed to prompt for input data, eg 'Time?' and to display results in the same way, eg 'LHA 296'. Again you get what you pay for, and results are provided more clearly, quickly and easily with these more expensive models. Whichever one is chosen, previous experience of calculators is unnecessary as manufacturers' instruction booklets provide all the required guidance, and proficiency is rapidly acquired after a little practice.

Apart from their value in astro-navigation, calculators will also make short work of coastal navigation problems. They will find course to steer to counteract tides; estimated positions; tidal heights and rates; course and speed made good; position by running fix, distance off, and a host of other solutions which save plotting and looking up tables.

**Astronomical Tables**

Complementary to the calculator are the special tables designed specifically for use with a simple pocket calculator. A single booklet contains all the required astronomical data for five years in a form which is fed directly into the calculator, without any interpolations, and produces a fix as the end result without drawing a single line on a chart, plotting sheet or graph paper.

The booklet is entitled, 'Compact Data for Navigation and

Astronomy for 1981 to 1985'. Written by Dr B. D. Yallop (HM Nautical Almanac Office), it is published as Royal Greenwich Observatory Bulletin No. 185; and is obtainable direct from the Observatory at a net cost of £3.

Most yachtsmen do carry a nautical almanac for the wealth of other information it provides, and they may accordingly prefer to use it for certain aspects of the astro-navigation process. For example, times of rising and setting and meridian passage may just as easily be found in an almanac as by calculator; and in this respect *Reed's Nautical Almanac* is perfectly satisfactory. Similarly, the correction tables for sextant sights in a nautical almanac may well be preferred by many yachtsmen.

Apart from these specific examples, a calculator provides all the required information more quickly and easily than traditional tables, and there will be no need to plot position lines to obtain a fix. As far as this book is concerned, traditional tables have earned, and passed into, honourable retirement.

# 2

# Principles of Astro-Navigation

The object of astro-navigation is to fix your position anywhere at sea. It is done in the same way as in coastal navigation, by the intersection of at least two position lines. The difference between coastal navigation and astro-navigation lies in the method of obtaining position lines. In coastal navigation (Fig 1), it is done by taking bearings of coastal landmarks, sea marks or radio beacons; and in astro-navigation by taking sextant sights of heavenly bodies such as the sun, moon, planets or stars.

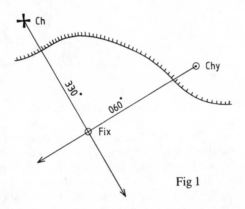

Fig 1

From a sextant sight we can obtain our position line relative to the heavenly body; but we cannot draw this position line on the chart as heavenly bodies are not marked on charts. They are too far away and their relative position changes throughout the day and the seasons as the earth rotates. However, the exact positions of certain heavenly bodies for any particular time anywhere in the world are given by astronomical tables. To fix our position all we have to do is:

Step 1 Determine our *estimated* position.

Step 2 Take a sextant sight from our *real* (unknown) position and record the exact time.

Step 3 Calculate from tables what the sextant sight would be if taken from the estimated position in step 1 at the time recorded in step 2.

The difference between the real sextant sight in step 2 and the calculated sight in step 3 enables us to draw our real position line on the chart. In this book we are not going to plot position lines on charts; they are only mentioned to help explain the principles of position fixing by astro-navigation.

The estimated position (EP) in step 1 is found from the course made good and distance travelled since the last fix (Fig 2). The traditional method of achieving this is by using the traverse tables in nautical almanacs or by direct plotting on a chart, but we shall do it quicker and more accurately by calculator.

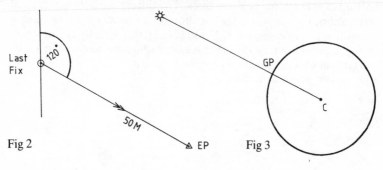

Fig 2      Fig 3

Having determined the EP we now calculate its bearing from the observed heavenly body and what the sextant sight would be if we really were at our EP. The difference between this calculated sight from our EP and the actual sight from our unknown position in step 2 tells us how far our real position line is from the EP. The following diagrams explain. In Fig 3 the circle represents the earth and C is the centre of the earth. A line drawn from C to the sun cuts the earth's surface at GP. At this point an observer would see the sun directly overhead. It is referred to as the **Geographical Position** (GP) of the heavenly body. Tables in nautical almanacs give the GP of a heavenly body at any time on any date but we shall again find it much quicker and easier by calculator.

Fig 4(a) shows what a sextant sight gives. An observer at Z would have his horizon represented by line AZB and his sextant would give the angle AZX between his horizon and the sun X, ie the sun's altitude. In Fig 4(a) the arc of the earth's surface GPZ forms a radius of the dotted circle on the earth's surface, centre GP. The sextant angle AZX giving the sun's altitude would be the same at any point on that circle. Thus a sextant sight gives a *position circle;* whereas the compass bearing used in coastal navigation (Fig 1) gives a position line.

In Fig 4(b) the observer's position Z is projected from the centre

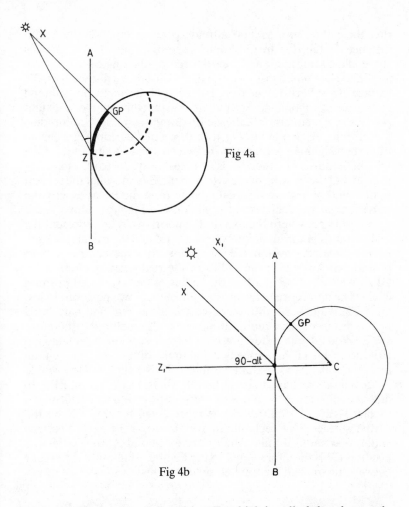

Fig 4a

Fig 4b

of the earth to a celestial position $Z_1$ which is called the observer's zenith. As the sun is so far away from earth, lines XZ from the sun to the observer, and $X_1C$ from the sun to the earth's centre can be regarded as parallel. Furthermore, angle $AZZ_1$ between the observer's horizon and zenith is a right angle. Thus angle $Z_1ZX$ equals 90° minus the sun's altitude AZX; and it also equals angle $Z_1CX_1$ as lines XZ and $X_1C$ are parallel. The expression 90° minus altitude is known mathematically as the co-altitude.

Arc GPZ is a terrestrial equivalent of the celestial angular distance of the sun from the observer's zenith and is accordingly called the **Zenith Distance**. But arc GPZ also forms a radius of the position circle, centre GP, in Fig 4(a); so we have now established

13

that the radius of a sextant altitude position circle is the zenith distance. In Fig 4(b) arc GPZ and its celestial equivalent $X_1Z_1$ both subtend the same angle at the earth's centre; this angle being the co-altitude. Thus zenith distance equals co-altitude, as distances on the surface of a sphere are measured in terms of the angle they subtend at its centre. It should now be understood that the radius of a sextant position circle equals both the zenith distance and the co-altitude.

Returning once more to Fig 4(a), the dotted position circle given by sextant sight AZX cannot be drawn on a chart as its centre (GP) may be hundreds or thousands of miles away. Instead, tables are used to find the bearing of the GP from the EP, and what the sextant sight would be if it were actually taken from the EP at exactly the same time as the real sextant sight AZX in Fig 4(a). This stage is shown in Fig 5, where the two dotted position circles represent the real sextant sight from unknown position Z and the calculated sight from estimated position EP. We know that the centre of both position circles is GP; the radius of the real position circle is arc GPZ; whilst arc GP Z EP is the radius of our estimated position circle. The difference between the radii of these two position circles, arc EPZ, equals the difference between the real and calculated zenith distances. But zenith distance equals co-altitude; therefore arc EPZ equals the difference between the real and calculated co-altitudes, which is numerically equal to the difference between the real and calculated sextant altitudes. This simplifies the whole process as all we have to do to find the distance of Z from EP is to find the difference in altitude between the real and calculated sextant sights. This difference is represented by arc EPZ on the earth's surface. But each minute of this arc on the earth's surface equals one nautical mile. The distance of point Z from estimated position EP is therefore equal to the number of minutes difference between the real and calculated sextant sights.

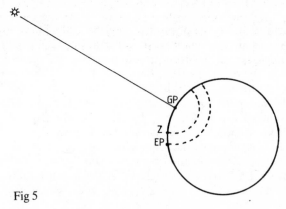

Fig 5

14

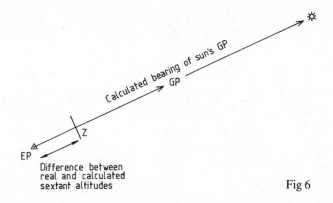

Fig 6

As mentioned above, we not only calculated the sun's altitude from our EP but also the bearing of the sun's GP from EP. From Fig 2 we can mark EP on a chart. Furthermore we can now draw through our EP the calculated bearing of the heavenly body. Using the latitude scale on the chart we can also mark position Z on that bearing as the number of minutes difference, expressed as nautical miles, between the calculated altitude at EP and the real altitude at Z (Fig 6).

Having plotted point Z on the chart it must be understood that this is not a fix. We only know at this stage that our true position is somewhere on the position circle, radius GPZ. Our true position line is, in fact, an arc of that circle passing through Z but it can be represented on our chart as a straight line. The position circle, radius GPZ, is so large that a small portion of it can be accurately represented as a straight line drawn through Z at right angles to the radius. In practice then, we just draw a line at the calculated bearing through our EP and mark off point Z on that line as the difference in minutes (nautical miles) between the calculated and true sextant altitudes. Our true position line can now be drawn through Z at right angles to the calculated bearing (Fig 7). To fix our position we just have to obtain a second position line (in the same way as the first) and their intersection provides a fix.

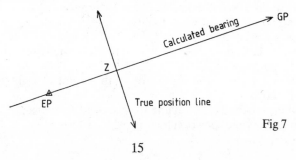

Fig 7

To sum up, the procedure is as follows:

1 Take sextant sight of heavenly body and record exact time.
2 Determine estimated position (EP) at time of sight.
3 From tables find geographical position (GP) of heavenly body at time of sight.
4 Calculate sextant altitude at EP and bearing of GP from EP.
5 Draw bearing through EP and mark position Z on bearing. Distance of Z from EP equals difference between real and calculated altitudes.
6 Draw true position line through Z at right angles to calculated bearing.
7 Take another sextant sight to give a fix at intersection of first and second position lines.

The following chapters will show how the traditional methods of completing steps 1–7 can be superseded by using a calculator and the special tables. There is no longer any need to pore through pages of complicated astronomical tables in nautical almanacs and sight reduction books, or to plot position lines on charts or graph paper.

Figures given in the following examples and exercises have been rounded to four decimal places but final answers are given to the nearest minute. This rounding will explain any differences in the last two decimal places between your own calculator results and those herein. Such differences have no practical significance as far as the end results are concerned and should be ignored.

## Summary

1 Sextant altitude of heavenly body gives true position circle.
2 Centre of circle is body's GP.
3 Radius of circle is zenith distance.
4 Zenith distance = 90° − altitude (co-altitude)
5 Tables give calculated altitude from EP and bearing of GP from EP.
6 Draw this bearing through EP.
7 True position circle cuts this bearing.
8 Distance (in miles) from EP to point of cut equals difference between true and calculated zenith distances.
9 This is numerically equal to difference (in minutes) between true and calculated sextant altitudes.
10 Using latitude scale, mark off this distance from EP along bearing.
11 Draw true position line through this point at right angles to bearing.
12 Obtain second position line from second sextant sight.
13 Intersection of position lines provides fix.

# 3

# Estimated Position

In most of the calculations in this book it is necessary to convert minutes and seconds into decimals of a degree or hour, and vice versa. Most scientific calculators have a special key for this purpose, but if not, minutes are decimalised by dividing by 60 and seconds by 3600.

| eg | 30′ | = | 30 ÷ 60 | = | 0.5 |
|----|-----|---|---------|---|-----|
| thus | 50° 30′ | = | 50°.5 | | |
| | 18 seconds | = | 18 ÷ 3600 | = | 0.0050 hours |
| | 10h30m18s GMT | = | 10 + 0.5 + 0.005 | | |
| | | = | 10.5050 GMT | | |

conversely:

| 10.5050 GMT | = | 10h (0.505 × 60)m |
|-------------|---|-------------------|
| | = | 10h30.3m |
| | = | 10h30m (0.3 × 60)s |
| | = | 10h30m18s GMT |

As outlined in the previous chapter, a sextant sight is the first step towards an astro-navigational fix. The sextant altitude must be recorded, together with the exact time of the sight and the log reading. Various corrections are applied to the sextant altitude and these are covered in Chapter 14.

The next step is to determine the yacht's estimated position (EP) at the recorded time of the sextant sight. The information required to calculate an estimated position is the course and distance made good since the last fix. The principle of the method is to convert course and distance into their rectangular co-ordinates. These are added to the last fix and their sum gives the estimated position. Fig 8 shows the course and distance made good (060°, 25 miles) to estimated position EP.

In mathematical parlance, any line of a given angle and length (eg a course and distance) is called a *polar co-ordinate*. If a rectangle is constructed about a polar co-ordinate so that it forms a diagonal of that rectangle, the sides of the rectangle are called its *rectangular co-ordinates* (Fig 9). Thus x and y are the rectangular co-ordinates of the course and distance travelled from the last fix to EP.

The P→R key on a calculator converts polar to rectangular co-

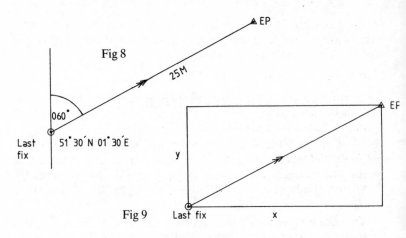

Fig 8

25M

060°

Last fix  51° 30′ N 01° 30′ E

y

Fig 9    Last fix    x

EP

EP

ordinates. If our course of 060° and distance travelled 25 miles are entered into a calculator, the P→R key produces the values x and y. But it is clear from Fig 9 that y is the difference in latitude (d.Lat) and x represents the difference in longitude (d.Long) between the fix and EP. By adding d.Lat and d.Long to the position of the last fix we obtain estimated position EP. The calculator formula for finding an estimated position is:

$$EP \quad \begin{matrix} \text{Lat} \\ \text{Long} \end{matrix} = \begin{matrix} \text{d.Lat + fix Lat} \\ \text{d.Long + fix Long} \end{matrix}$$

The calculator sequence is:

i   Input:    25    60    P→R
ii  Output:   y co-ordinate   12.5000
              x co-ordinate   21.6506

The calculator gives the rectangular co-ordinates of our course and distance as 12.5 and 21.6506. As the unit of length entered into the calculator was miles (25M), so is the output given in miles. But one mile equals one minute of latitude. Thus the y co-ordinate which gives d.Lat equals 12.5′. The yacht has therefore travelled 12.5′ north from the last fix and the latitude of EP is accordingly 51° 30′ + 12.5′ = 51° 42.5′N. However, one nautical mile does not equal one minute of longitude (except on the equator). Distance x, which represents the difference in longitude, is 21.6506 miles and is called the **Departure**. Thus departure may be defined as difference in longitude expressed in nautical miles. But we need to have it expressed in minutes of longitude to determine our estimated position. The formula for converting departure into longitude is:

d.Long  =  departure/cos mean Lat

18

Mean Lat is the average of the latitudes of the fix and EP; and is most easily found by halving d.Lat and adding it to the latitude of the fix. The formula now becomes:

d.Long = departure/cos (d.Lat/2 + fix Lat)

In practice d.Lat and departure are stored in the calculator memory as soon as they appear on display. If the first display (12.5) giving d.Lat is decimalised and stored in memory 1, departure (21.6506) in memory 2, and the latitude of the last fix (decimalised 51.5) in memory 3; then

d.Long = memory 2 ÷ cos (memory 1 ÷ 2 + memory 3)
= 21.6506 ÷ cos (0.2083 ÷ 2 + 51.5)
= 34.8591′

Thus the longitude of EP is 01° 30′ + 35′ = 02° 05′E.
Estimated position EP is accordingly 51° 42.5′N 02° 05′E.

Now consider what happens if the situation is reversed. The last fix becomes 51° 42.5′ N 02° 05′ E and the yacht sails 25 miles on a reciprocal course of 240° (Fig 10). The calculator sequence is 25 240 P→R and the resultant rectangular co-ordinates are −12.5000 and −21.6506. The figures must obviously be the same as before as d.Lat and d.Long are the same, but both are now displayed as negative quantities. The reason for the difference is that whereas the yacht travelled north east before, it is now travelling south west, which is just what the calculator tells us by displaying a minus sign.

This gives a fundamental and essential rule for calculator workings:

North and east are *positive*. South and west are *negative*.

This applies equally for the input and output sides of a calculator. Thus the results from Fig 10 give the new EP as 12.5 miles south and 21.65 miles west of our fix. Therefore:

d.Lat = −12.5′
d.Long = −35′
EP = 51° 42.5′ + (−12.5′) = 51° 30′
02° 05′ + (−35′) = 01° 30′

As both figures for EP are positive, the estimated position EP is 51° 30′N 01° 30′E.

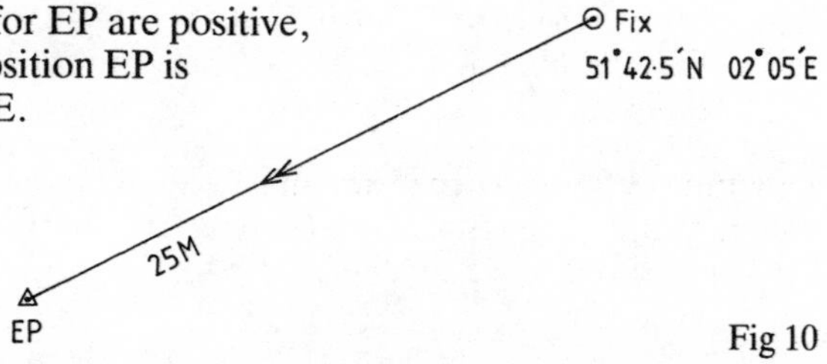

Fig 10

19

*Example*
From position 51° 30'S 01° 30'E, course and distance made good 060°, 25 miles. Find the estimated position.

From the previous calculations we know that:

| | | |
|---|---|---|
| d.Lat | = | 12.5' |
| d.Long | = | 35' |
| EP Lat | = | −51° 30' + 12.5' |
| | = | −51° 17.5' |
| EP Long | = | 01° 30' + 35' |
| | = | 02° 05' |

Estimated position is <u>51° 17.5'S 02° 05'E</u>.

From position 51° 30'S 01° 30'W, same course and distance.

| | | |
|---|---|---|
| EP Lat | = | −51° 30' + 12.5' |
| | = | −51° 17.5' |
| EP Long | = | −01° 30' + 35' |
| | = | −00° 55' |

Estimated position is <u>51° 17.5'S 00° 55'W</u>

It might be thought quicker, at first glance, to plot these examples on a chart or graph paper rather than use a calculator, but in practice the chart or paper work would be far more complicated. The examples given are for course and distance made good but these are not necessarily the same as course steered and distance logged. The latter are affected by tidal streams and the yacht may have been tacking to make good a course of 060°. In practice the course and distance made good are found by converting all the courses steered and tides encountered into rectangular co-ordinates and adding them. Their total gives course and distance made good. It would be a very tiresome exercise to plot this on a chart if several different courses and tides were involved, as the following examples show.

*Example*
1 A yacht, tacking, steered the following courses and logged distances: 015° 5M, 105° 5M, 025° 10M, 115° 10M. Find the course and distance made good.

By calculator:

| Input | Key | Display | |
|---|---|---|---|
| 5 | | | |
| 15 | P→R | 4.8296 | memory 1 |
| | x-y | 1.2941 | memory 2 |

| Input | Key | Display | |
|-------|-----|---------|---|
| 5 | | | |
| 105 | P→R | −1.2941 | + memory 1 |
| | x-y | 4.8296 | + memory 2 |
| 10 | | | |
| 25 | P→R | 9.0631 | + memory 1 |
| | x-y | 4.2262 | + memory 2 |
| 10 | | | |
| 115 | P→R | −4.2262 | + memory 1 |
| | x-y | 9.0631 | + memory 2 |
| | recall 1 | 8.3724 | d.Lat |
| | recall 2 | 19.4130 | departure |

We now know d.Lat and departure. These can be converted, if required, into course and distance made good by using the inverse PR key (R→P).

| | recall 1 | 8.3724 | d.Lat |
|---|----------|--------|-------|
| | recall 2 | 19.4130 | departure |
| | R→P | 21.1415 | distance made good |
| | x-y | 66.6704 | course made good |

Thus the course and distance made good is 067°, 21 miles but in practice we only need to know d.Lat and departure. The same procedure is used for the prevailing tides. All the courses steered, distances logged, charted tidal sets and drifts are converted into rectangular co-ordinates and added.

2 From position 51° 30′ S 01° 30′ E, a yacht tacked 340° for one hour at 8 knots, 250° for one hour at 10 knots, 340° for one hour at 4 knots. Tides were: 1st hour 020° 2k; 2nd hour 030° 1k; 3rd hour 200° 1.5k. Find the estimated position.
The calculator sequence is:

| 8 | 340 | P→R | memory 1 | x-y | memory 2 |
|-----|-----|-----|------------|-----|------------|
| 10 | 250 | P→R | + memory 1 | x-y | + memory 2 |
| 4 | 340 | P→R | + memory 1 | x-y | + memory 2 |
| 2 | 20 | P→R | + memory 1 | x-y | + memory 2 |
| 1 | 30 | P→R | + memory 1 | x-y | + memory 2 |
| 1.5 | 200 | P→R | + memory 1 | x-y | + memory 2 |

| recall 1 | 9.1920 | d.Lat | memory 1 |
|----------|----------|-----------|----------|
| recall 2 | −12.8302 | departure | memory 2 |

d.Lat and departure are now stored in memory. Original latitude is now decimalised and stored in memory 3 and the calculation proceeds:

21

| EP Lat | = | memory 3 + memory 1 (decimalised) |
| | = | −51.5 + 0.1532 |
| | = | −51°.3468 = −51° 21′ (negative answer means South) |
| d.Long′ | = | memory 2 ÷ cos (memory 1 ÷ 2 + memory 3) |
| | = | −20.5756′ |
| EP Long | = | 01° 30′ (decimalised) + d.Long (decimalised) |
| | = | 1.5 + (−0.3429) |
| | = | 1°.1571 = 01° 9.4′ (positive answer means East) |

Estimated position is 51° 21′S 01° 09′E

**Summary**

North and East are positive. South and West are negative

Courses steered
Distances logged $\Big\}$ Total of rectangular = $\Big\{$ d.Lat
Tidal sets co-ordinates departure
Tidal drifts

| d.Long | = | departure/cos mean Lat |
| | = | departure/cos (d.Lat/2 + fix Lat) |
| EP | = | fix Lat + d.Lat |
| | = | fix Long + d.Long |

*Exercise 1* (Answers in Appendix C)
1 From position 30°N 15°W, a yacht made good a course and distance of 350°, 100 miles, Find the yacht's EP.
2 A yacht steers 130° for 240 miles from position 2° 02′N 45° 25′E. What is her EP?
3 From position 3° 40′N 6° 10′E, a yacht makes good a course of 209° for 400 miles. what is her EP?
4 A yacht in position 51° 20′N 1° 34′E steered a course of 143° for the next four hours and logged a distance of 21.2 miles. The tides affecting the yacht each hour were: 208° at 3.1 knots; 201° at 3 knots; 213° at 1.3 knots; and 050° at 1.3 knots. Find yacht's EP.
5 A yacht in position 54° 04.8′N 04° 58.7′E logged the following courses during the next 24 hours:
270°    30 miles; tidal set 215° drift 4 miles.
180°    24 miles; tidal set 035° drift 6 miles.
265°    10 miles; tidal set 220° drift 1.6 miles.
175°     8 miles; tidal set 225° drift 2.3 miles.
220°    25 miles; tidal set 047° drift 5.8 miles.
Find the yacht's EP.

# 4

# Geographical Position

Chapter 3 showed how to calculate the estimated position at which a sextant sight was taken. The next step towards obtaining an astro-navigational fix is to find the geographical position of the observed heavenly body at the time of sextant sight. Referring back to Fig 3, the geographical position (GP) is a terrestrial equivalent of the celestial position of the body. Like other terrestrial positions, the geographical position can be expressed in terms of latitude and longitude. These values can be found in astronomical tables but they are given special names as they relate to a celestial rather than terrestrial position. Celestial latitude is called **Declination** and celestial longitude is called **Greenwich Hour Angle**.

Declination is measured north or south of the celestial equator (called the equinoctial) in the same way as terrestrial latitude. Greenwich Hour Angle, however, differs from terrestrial longitude insofar as it is only measured *westwards* from Greenwich, so its value is expressed in three-figure notation (0°–360°).

## Sun and Planets

Declination (Dec) and Greenwich Hour Angle (GHA) are found from the monthly tables of calculator data in RGO Bulletin 185. The formula for GHA is:

$$\text{GHA} = 15((((a_4x + a_3)x + a_2)x + a_1)x + a_0 + \text{GMT})$$

where GMT = time in hours
x = (date + GMT/24)/32

*Example*

Find GHA Sun, 12 December 1981 at 1800 GMT.
By calculator:

$$x \ = \ (12 + 18 \div 24) \div 32$$
$$= \ 0.3984 \quad \text{(memory 5)}$$

RGO tables, see Appendix B

$$a_4 \ = \ 0.01015 \text{ (memory 4)}$$
$$a_3 \ = \ 0.02644 \text{ (memory 3)}$$
$$a_2 \ = \ -0.09039 \text{ (memory 2)}$$
$$a_1 \ = \ -0.19238 \text{ (memory 1)}$$
$$a_0 \ = \ 12.19132 \text{ (memory 0)}$$

Check sum of memories 0–4 = 11.945140

GHA  =  15 × ((((memory 4 × memory 5 + memory 3) ×
memory 5 + memory 2) × memory 5 + memory 1) ×
memory 5 + memory 0 + 18)

   =  451.5337

Any answer greater than 360 must have multiples of 360 subtracted.

GHA Sun  =  451.5337 – 360
      =  *91.5337*

Declination is found in the same way but the formula is shorter:

$$\text{Dec} \ = \ (((a_4x + a_3)x + a_2)x + a_1)x + a_0$$

*Example*

Same date and time; find declination of Venus.

RGO tables, see Appendix B

$$x \ = \ (12 + 18 \div 24) \div 32$$
$$= \ 0.3984 \text{ (already stored in memory 5)}$$

$$a_4 \ = \ -0.2605 \text{ (memory 4)}$$
$$a_3 \ = \ -1.5674 \text{ (memory 3)}$$
$$a_2 \ = \ 3.2525 \text{ (memory 2)}$$
$$a_1 \ = \ 6.4137 \text{ (memory 1)}$$
$$a_0 \ = \ -24.4064 \text{ (memory 0)}$$

Check sum of memories 0–4 = −16.5681

Dec Venus  =  (((memory 4 × memory 5 + memory 3) ×
memory 5 + memory 2) × memory 5 +
memory 1) × memory 5 + memory 0

     =  −21.4403

The negative answer means that the declination of Venus is
*21°.4403 South*. Positive answers mean north declination.

**Moon**

Declination and Greenwich Hour Angle of the Moon are both found from the same formula:

GHA, Dec Moon $= (a_2x + a_1)x + a_0$

where $x = $ GMT/24

*Example*
Same date and time; find GHA and Dec Moon.

RGO tables, see Appendix B
x $=$ 18 ÷ 24
$=$ 0.75 (memory 1)
GHA $=$ (0.0734 × memory 1 + 344.6640) × memory 1 + 351.7425
$=$ 610.2818 (−360)
$=$ *250.2818*

*Similarly*
Dec $=$ (−0.7981 × memory 1 + 1.3845) × memory 1 + 21.3304
$=$ 21.9198
Declination Moon is *21°.9198 North.*


**Stars**

Declination of stars is found in a similar way to the sun, moon and planets. But the Greenwich Hour Angle of stars is not quite the same. 'Longitude' of stars is measured westwards from a special celestial meridian which passes through the constellation Aries. The value obtained is called the **Sidereal Hour Angle** (SHA) of the star, and is constant for all practical purposes.

Unfortunately for us, Aries is not the celestial projection of Greenwich. This means that its position relative to Greenwich is changing all the time as the earth rotates. So the first step in finding the Greenwich Hour Angle of a star (GHA*) is to find the Greenwich Hour Angle of Aries (GHAγ). Then:

GHA* $=$ GHAγ + SHA

The formula for finding GHAγ is:

GHAγ $=$ A + 0.985647x + 15 GMT

where x $=$ date + GMT/24

*Example*
Same date and time; find GHAγ.

    RGO tables, see Appendix B

| | | |
|---|---|---|
| A | = | 68.7810 |
| x | = | $12 + 18 \div 24$ |
| | = | 12.75 (memory 1) |
| GHAγ | = | $68.7810 + 0.985647 \times$ memory $1 + 15 \times 18$ |
| | = | *351.3480* (memory 2) |

The formula for sidereal hour angle and declination is:

SHA, Dec   =    $a_0 + 0.0001 (a_1 + a_2 x)$

where x is the same as for GHAγ.

*Example*
Same time and date; find GHA* and Dec Sirius.

    RGO tables, see Appendix B

| | | |
|---|---|---|
| SHA | = | $258.9072 + 0.0001 (0 + -0.6 \times$ memory 1) |
| | = | *258.9064* (memory 3) |
| GHA* | = | GHAγ + SHA |
| | = | memory 2 + memory 3 |
| | = | $610.2544 (-360)$ |
| | = | *250.2544* |
| Dec (S) | = | $16.6879 + 0.0001 (24 + 0.7 \times$ memory 1) |
| | = | *16°.6912 S* |

## Summary

| | | | | |
|---|---|---|---|---|
| GP | { | latitude | = | Dec |
| Sun, Moon, planets | { | longitude | = | GHA |

| | | | | |
|---|---|---|---|---|
| GP Stars | { | latitude | = | Dec |
| | { | longitude | = | GHAγ + SHA |
| | | | = | GHA* |

| | | |
|---|---|---|
| Dec | = | celestial latitude (N+ S−) |
| GHA | = | celestial longitude (0° – 360°W from Greenwich meridian) |
| GHAγ | = | celestial longitude Aries (0° – 360°W from Greenwich meridian) |
| SHA | = | celestial longitude star (0° – 360°W from Aries) |

*Sun and Planets*

GHA = $15((((a_4x + a_3)x + a_2)x + a_1)x + a_0 + GMT)$

Dec = $(((a_4x + a_3)x + a_2)x + a_1)x + a_0$

x = $(date + GMT/24)/32$

*Moon*

GHA, Dec = $(a_2x + a_1)x + a_0$

x = $GMT/24$

*Stars*

GHA* = $GHA\gamma + SHA$

GHA$\gamma$ = $A + 0.985647x + 15\ GMT$

SHA, Dec = $a_0 + 0.0001\ (a_1 + a_2x)$

x = $date + GMT/24$

**Exercise 2** (Answers in Appendix C)

1 Find GHA and declination of the Sun on 4 December 1981 at
  i   09h16m30s GMT
  ii  13h20m15s GMT
2 Find GHA and declination of Venus on 10 December 1981 at
  i   14h58m38s GMT
  ii  16h42m39s GMT
3 Find GHA and declination of the Moon on
  i   12 December 1981 at 07h43m29s GMT
  ii  5 November 1981 at 21h05m47s GMT
4 Find GHA and declination of Arcturus on 22 September 1981 at
  1847 GMT.
5 Find GHA and declination of Sirius on 5 March 1981 at
  19h14m07s GMT.

# 5

# Calculated Altitude and Azimuth

Before proceeding further it may be helpful to recapitulate what has been achieved so far:

1 Sextant sight of heavenly body from unknown position.
2 Calculation of EP at time of sextant sight.
3 Calculation of body's GP at time of sight.

With this information we can now proceed to step four, which is to calculate what the sextant altitude would be if we really were at our EP; and the bearing of GP from EP. These calculations use the same formulae, irrespective of the body observed.

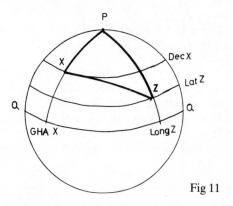

Fig 11

The formulae are derived by spherical trigonometry from the concept shown in Fig 11. This represents the terrestrial sphere, with P as the pole, Q as the equator, X as a heavenly body's GP and Z as the observer's EP. These points form what is known as the PZX triangle. The arcs of the meridians from the pole through X and Z to the equator equal 90° of latitude. Thus PX equals 90° minus declination and PZ equals 90° minus EP latitude. XZ is the zenith distance and angle PZX is the bearing of GP from EP. Angle XPZ is the difference in longitude between EP and GP. This difference is called the **Local Hour Angle** (LHA) of the body concerned. It is called local as it is the 'local longitude' of the observed body from the observer's position.

We can find the values PX, PZ and angle XPZ from our previous calculations of EP and GP. The next task is to find zenith distance XZ and bearing PZX. The original formulae for finding these use special trigonometrical ratios called haversines. Many navigators still use them and haversine tables are accordingly included in some nautical almanacs.

As shown in Chapter 2, zenith distance equals co-altitude, which is defined as 90° minus altitude. Thus the haversine formula for calculating zenith distance also finds the calculated altitude; and this led to the introduction of sight reduction tables in which the haversine formulae are pre-calculated to give the calculated altitude and bearing for every degree of latitude, minute of declination and degree of LHA. These tables, or the original haversine method, are the traditional ways of obtaining an astro-navigational fix but they are now being challenged by the pocket calculator. Haversine formulae for solving the PZX triangle can be adapted for use with calculators and provide navigators with a much quicker and easier way of finding the calculated altitude and bearing.

### Calculated Altitude

The formula for calculated altitude is:

$$\sin Hc = \sin Lat \sin Dec + \cos Lat \cos Dec \cos LHA$$

where Hc = calculated altitude
Lat = latitude of estimated position (EP Lat)
Dec = declination of observed heavenly body
LHA = local hour angle of body

Local hour angle (LHA) is the difference in longitude between EP and GP, ie the 'local longitude' of the observed body measured westwards from EP to GP. The calculator formula for finding LHA is accordingly:

$$LHA = GHA + EP \text{ longitude}$$

The calculator rule of always naming west and south as negative avoids the complication found in traditional formulae of having to choose between different signs. For example, the traditional formula is LHA = GHA $^{+\text{east}}_{-\text{west}}$ EP longitude. As west and south are always given a negative prefix in calculator use, the correct sign is automatically entered into the particular calculation, as the following examples show.

29

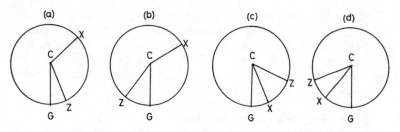

| (a) | (b) | (c) | (d) |

Fig 12

*Examples*
The following examples are illustrated in Fig 12,

    where CG is the Greenwich meridian
            CZ is the EP meridian
            CX is the sun's GP meridian

a) At EP 55°N 5°E; GHA Sun 240°. Find LHA.

$$
\begin{aligned}
\text{LHA} &= \text{GHA} + \text{EP Long} \\
&= 240 + 5 \\
&= 245°
\end{aligned}
$$

| EP Long is angle GCZ | = | 5°E |
| GHA is external angle GCX | = | 240° |
| LHA is external angle ZCX | = | 245° |

b) At EP 55°N 10°W; GHA Sun 240°. Find LHA.

$$
\begin{aligned}
\text{LHA} &= 240 + (-10) \\
&= 230°
\end{aligned}
$$

Remember that West is always negative and East is always positive.

| EP Long is angle GCZ | = | 10°W |
| GHA is external angle GCX | = | 240° |
| LHA is external angle ZCX | = | 230° |

c) At EP 55°N 50°E; GHA Sun 350°. Find LHA.

$$
\begin{aligned}
\text{LHA} &= 350 + 50 \\
&= 400\ (-360) \\
&= 40°
\end{aligned}
$$

Multiples of 360 are subtracted to make LHA less than 360.

| EP Long is angle GCZ | = | 50°E |
| GHA is external angle GCX | = | 350° |
| LHA is angle ZCX | = | 40° |

d) At EP 55°N 50°W; GHA Sun 030°. Find LHA.

LHA $=$ 30 + (−50)
$\phantom{LHA} =$ −20 (+360)
$\phantom{LHA} =$ 340°

Add 360 to negative answers to make LHA positive.

EP Long is angle GCZ $\quad = \quad$ 50°W
GHA is angle GCX $\quad = \quad$ 30°
LHA is external angle ZCX $\quad = \quad$ 340°

Now proceed to find some calculated altitudes.

*Examples*
1  EP 50°N 17°W; GHA Sun 313°, Dec 19°N.
   Find calculated altitude.

LHA $=$ GHA + EP Long
$\phantom{LHA} =$ 313 + (−17)
$\phantom{LHA} =$ 296

sin Hc $=$ sin Lat sin Dec + cos Lat cos Dec cos LHA
$\phantom{sin Hc} =$ sin 50 × sin 19 + cos 50 × cos 19 × cos 296
$\phantom{sin Hc} =$ 0.5158
inv sin $=$ 31°.0528

*Calculated altitude Hc = 31°.0528*

2  EP 50°S 150°E; GHA Sun 280°, Dec 12°S.

LHA $=$ 280 + 150
$\phantom{LHA} =$ 430 (−360)
$\phantom{LHA} =$ 70
sin Hc $=$ sin(−50) × sin(−12) + cos(−50) × cos(−12) × cos 70
$\phantom{sin Hc} =$ 0.3743
*Hc* $=$ *21°.9818*

**Calculated Bearing (Azimuth)**

The next step after calculating the altitude from EP is to calculate the bearing of GP from EP. This bearing is called the body's **azimuth** (Az). It is found by converting rectangular co-ordinates x and y into their polar co-ordinate angle.

x $=$ cos Lat sin Dec − sin Lat cos Dec cos LHA
y $=$ −cos Dec sin LHA
Az $=$ polar co-ordinate angle

31

The calculator sequence is:

1 Calculate x co-ordinate
2 Calculate y co-ordinate
3 Convert x and y into their polar co-ordinates
4 Polar co-ordinate angle is the azimuth

*Examples*
1 Same figures as previous example 1.

EP Lat  =  50  memory 1
Dec  =  19  memory 2
LHA  =  296 memory 3

cos memory 1 × sin memory 2 – sin memory 1 × cos memory 2 ×
cos memory 3  =  −0.1082
−cos memory 2 × sin memory 3  =  0.8498
−0.1082  0.8498  R→P  =  0.8567  97.2589

*Az  =  097°.2589*

2 Same figures as previous example 2.

EP Lat  =  −50
Dec  =  −12
LHA  =  70

$\cos(-50) \times \sin(-12) - \sin(-50) \times \cos(-12) \times \cos 70 = 0.1226$
$-\cos(-12) \times \sin 70 = -0.9192$
0.1226  −0.9192  R→P  =  0.9273  −82.4029

Az  =  −82.4029 (+360)
   =  *277°.5971*

3 EP 51° 30′N 02°E; 15 December 1981 at 1700 GMT. Calculate
altitude and azimuth of Venus.

RGO tables, see Appendix B

x  =  (15 + 17 ÷ 24) ÷ 32
   =  0.4909 (memory 1)

GHA  =  15 × (((((0.03408 × memory 1 + 0.2387) ×
        memory 1 + 0.59659) × memory 1 + 0.21447) ×
        memory 1 + 8.87676 + 17)
     =  392.3402 (−360)
     =  32.3402

LHA  =  32.3402 + 2
     =  34.3402 (memory 3)

32

$$\text{Dec} = (((-0.2605 \times \text{memory} 1 + -1.5674) \times \text{memory} 1 +$$
$$3.2525) \times \text{memory} 1 + 6.4137) \times \text{memory} 1 +$$
$$-24.4064$$
$$= -20.6748 \,(\text{memory} 2)$$

EP Lat $=$ 51.5 (memory 1)

sin Hc $=$ sin memory 1 $\times$ sin memory 2 + cos memory 1 $\times$ cos memory 2 $\times$ cos memory 3

$\quad\quad = 0.2046$

Hc $= 11°.8060$

*Calculated altitude $= 11°.8060$*

x $=$ cos memory 1 $\times$ sin memory 2 $-$ sin memory 1 $\times$ cos memory 2 $\times$ cos memory 3

$\quad = -0.8244$

y $= -$cos memory 2 $\times$ sin memory 3

$\quad = -0.5278$

R$\rightarrow$P $= -147.3720 \,(+360)$

$\quad = 212°.6280$

*Azimuth $= 212°.6$*

## Summary

LHA $=$ local longitude of GP measured westwards from EP

$\quad\quad = $ GHA + EP longitude

Hc $=$ calculated altitude

sin Hc $=$ sin Lat sin Dec + cos Lat cos Dec cos LHA

Azimuth $=$ polar co-ordinate angle of rectangular co-ordinates x & y

x $=$ cos Lat sin Dec $-$ sin Lat cos Dec cos LHA

y $= -$cos Dec sin LHA

Az $=$ R$\rightarrow$P angle

## Exercise 3 (Answers in Appendix C)

1  On 17 October 1981 at 18h50m13s GMT, in EP 11° 07′S  97° 42′W, calculate the altitude and azimuth of the sun.

2  On 6 December 1981 at 15h37m42s GMT, in EP 51° 11′N  3° 01′E, calculate the altitude and azimuth of Venus.

3  On 15 October 1981 at 0530 GMT, in EP 51° 11′N  01°58′E, calculate the altitude and azimuth of the moon.

4  On 1 August 1981 at 18h40m52s GMT, in EP 38° 45′N  03° 27′E, calculate the altitude and azimuth of Antares.

5  On 9 April 1981 at 21h01m36s GMT, in EP 45°N  03°16′W, calculate the altitude and azimuth of Vega.

# 6

# First Position Line

Figs 4–7 in Chapter 2 show how an astro-navigational position line is found. A sextant altitude only provides a position circle; the centre of the circle being the observed body's GP. The actual position is somewhere on the circumference of that circle. But, as explained in Chapter 2, a position circle is too large to be drawn on a chart. Instead we have to calculate what the sextant altitude would have been if we really were at the estimated position instead of our actual unknown position. The difference between the real sextant altitude from our unknown position and the calculated altitude from EP equals the distance of our actual position circle from the EP circle (Fig 5).

Although it is not practicable to draw position circles on a chart we can mark our EP on a chart. We also know from Chapter 5 how to calculate, not only our EP altitude, but the bearing (Az) of GP from EP. So we can now mark EP on a chart and draw a line through it representing the bearing of GP from EP (Fig 6). This bearing represents a radius (length GP EP) of our estimated position circle passing through EP; but the radius of any position circle equals the zenith distance. The point where our actual position circle cuts the bearing can therefore be marked on the bearing as the difference between the real and calculated zenith distances, which is numerically the same as the difference in minutes between the real and calculated altitudes. Fig 5 shows this difference as arc EPZ and it is marked off as shown in Fig 6 from EP along the bearing EP GP to point Z.

The distance from EP to Z is called the **intercept** and is marked on the bearing, using the latitude scale, as the number of minutes difference between the real and calculated altitudes. In relation to EP, point Z may be nearer to or further away from GP; so an intercept is traditionally expressed as *towards* if it is nearer to GP (Figs 6 & 7) or *away* if it is beyond EP (Fig 13). If the real sextant altitude is greater than the calculated altitude, the intercept is towards. If it is less, the intercept is away from EP.

Our real position circle, radius GP Z, passes through Z and we are somewhere on the circumference of that circle. But as we must be somewhere near EP we can represent our arc of this enormous circle as a straight position line drawn through Z at right angles to

34

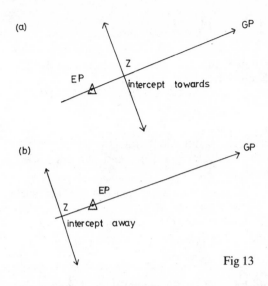

(a)

Z

EP

intercept towards

GP

(b)

GP

EP

Z

intercept away

Fig 13

the bearing EP GP (Figs 7 & 13). In the traditional method of obtaining a fix, this is exactly what is done. EP, Az and position line through Z are drawn on a chart or plotting sheet, or to scale on graph paper. A second sextant sight enables a second position line to be drawn and their intersection gives a fix. In this book we are not going to fix our position in this traditional way; we shall do it all by calculator.

By calculator we only need to find the difference in altitudes. In the previous chapter we found the calculated altitude Hc and bearing Az of the observed body from our EP. The actual sextant sight from our real unknown position is called the **true observed altitude** (Ho). All we have to do at this stage is record the bearing (Az) of GP from EP and the difference between Ho and Hc. This difference is the intercept and is represented by the symbol p. Thus:

$$p \ = \ Ho - Hc$$

A positive intercept is the same as the traditional intercept towards, whilst a negative intercept corresponds to the traditional intercept away. Another difference from the traditional method is that calculator intercepts are expressed as decimals of a degree instead of in minutes.

*Examples*
1 A sextant sight of star Vega gave a true observed altitude of 30° 15′. The calculated altitude and azimuth were 30° 12′, 210°. Find the intercept.

35

$$\text{Intercept p} \quad = \quad \text{Ho} - \text{Hc}$$
$$= \quad 30°\,15' - 30°\,12'$$
$$= \quad 3'$$

By calculator, all our altitudes are decimalised so the calculation really becomes:

$$\text{p} \quad = \quad 30°.25 - 30°.20$$
$$= \quad 0°.05$$

2 A sextant sight of star Aldebaran gave a true observed altitude of 15° 09′. The calculated altitude and azimuth were 15° 14′, 170°. Find the intercept.

$$\text{p} \quad = \quad 15°\,09'\ (\text{decimalised}) - 15°\,14'\ (\text{decimalised})$$
$$= \quad 15°.15 - 15°.2333$$
$$= \quad -0°.0833$$

Note that p may be positive or negative and must be stored as such in the calculator's memory.

It should be stated at this stage that all sextant sights taken by navigators must have various corrections applied before they can be used as the true observed altitude Ho. For the sake of simplicity, these corrections are assumed to have been applied, and all sextant altitudes given in the examples and exercises should be regarded as value Ho. Chapter 14 covers all the corrections and gives calculator formulae for converting an observed sextant altitude into the true observed altitude Ho.

**Summary**

$$\text{Intercept p} \quad = \quad \text{difference between observed and calculated altitudes}$$
$$= \quad \text{Ho} - \text{Hc}$$

Answer may be positive or negative

**Exercise 4** (Answers in Appendix C)

1 A sextant sight of the sun gave a true altitude of 81° 15′. The calculated altitude was 81°.2629. Find the intercept.
2 When the sextant altitude of Venus was 15° 35′ the calculated altitude was 15°.1584. Find the intercept.
3 The true altitude of the moon was 39° 51′; calculated altitude 39°.9365. Find the intercept.
4 A sextant sight of Antares gave a true altitude of 24° 01′. The calculated altitude was 23°.7126. Find the intercept.
5 A sextant sight of Vega gave a true observed altitude of 75° 39′. The calculated altitude was 75°.5240. Find the intercept.

# 7

# Calculation of the Fix

The last two chapters have shown how a single sextant sight from an unknown position can lead to an intercept and azimuth from the estimated position. If the same process is repeated for a second sight, a second intercept and azimuth are obtained and a fix can be calculated. Traditionally, the intercepts (p) and azimuths (Az) are plotted to give position lines, and the fix is their point of intersection. However, all that paper work can be avoided by using a calculator.

The calculator formulae for obtaining a fix are:

$$A = \cos^2 Az_1 + \cos^2 Az_2 + \cos^2 Az_3 + \cos^2 Az_4 \dots\dots\dots\dots\dots$$

where $Az_1$ is the calculated bearing of the first sight
$Az_2$ is the calculated bearing of the second sight
$Az_3$ is the calculated bearing of the third sight (if taken)

Any successive sight is treated in the same way by adding to the sum of the previous sights.

The same pattern is repeated for the following formulae:

$$B = \cos Az_1 \sin Az_1 + \cos Az_2 \sin Az_2 \dots\dots\dots\dots\dots\dots\dots$$
$$C = \sin^2 Az_1 + \sin^2 Az_2 \dots\dots\dots\dots\dots\dots\dots\dots\dots\dots$$
$$D = p_1 \cos Az_1 + p_2 \cos Az_2 \dots\dots\dots\dots\dots\dots\dots\dots\dots$$
$$E = p_1 \sin Az_1 + p_2 \sin Az_2 \dots\dots\dots\dots\dots\dots\dots\dots\dots$$

Check that $A + C$ = the number of sights taken.

Then form value G from:

$$G = AC - B^2$$

Values A to G are stored in memories and the fix is calculated as follows:

$$d.Lat = (DC - EB)/G$$
$$d.Long = (AE - BD)/(G \cos EP\ Lat)$$

$$Fix = EP\ Lat + d.Lat$$
$$EP\ Long + d.Long$$

*Example*

At EP 55°N 05°E, the following star sights were calculated:

1  Vega, intercept 0°.05, azimuth 210°
2  Aldebaran, intercept −0°.0833, azimuth 170°

Fix the yacht's position.

$$
\begin{aligned}
A &= \text{Vega}\cos^2 Az + \text{Aldebaran}\cos^2 Az \\
&= \cos^2 210 + \cos^2 170 \\
&= 1.7198
\end{aligned}
$$

$$
\begin{aligned}
B &= \cos Az_1 \sin Az_1 + \cos Az_2 \sin Az_2 \\
&= \cos 210 \times \sin 210 + \cos 170 \times \sin 170 \\
&= 0.2620
\end{aligned}
$$

$$
\begin{aligned}
C &= \sin^2 Az_1 + \sin^2 Az_2 \\
&= \sin^2 210 + \sin^2 170 \\
&= 0.2802
\end{aligned}
$$

Now check that $A + C$ = the number of sights taken. In this example $A + C$ should equal 2, confirming that A and C were calculated correctly:

$$1.7198 \quad + \quad 0.2802 \quad = \quad 2$$

$$
\begin{aligned}
G &= AC - B^2 \\
&= 1.7198 \times 0.2802 - (0.2620)^2 \\
&= 0.4132
\end{aligned}
$$

$$
\begin{aligned}
D &= p_1 \cos Az_1 + p_2 \cos Az_2 \\
&= 0.05 \times \cos 210 + -0.0833 \times \cos 170 \\
&= 0.0387
\end{aligned}
$$

$$
\begin{aligned}
E &= p_1 \sin Az_1 + p_2 \sin Az_2 \\
&= 0.05 \times \sin 210 + -0.0833 \times \sin 170 \\
&= -0.0395
\end{aligned}
$$

As each value A to G is found, it is stored in the calculator's memory.

The next step is to find the difference in latitude and longitude of the unknown position from the estimated position. A fix can then be obtained from the formula:

$$
\begin{aligned}
\text{Fix} &= \text{EP Lat} + \text{d.Lat} \\
& \quad\ \text{EP Long} + \text{d.Long}
\end{aligned}
$$

$$
\begin{aligned}
\text{d.Lat} &= (DC - EB)/G \\
&= (0.0387 \times 0.2802 - -0.0395 \times 0.2620) \div 0.4132 \\
&= 0.0513
\end{aligned}
$$

| d.Long | = | $(AE - BD)/(G \cos EP \, Lat)$ |
|--------|---|------------------------------------|
|        | = | $(1.7198 \times -0.0395 - 0.2620 \times 0.0387) \div$ |
|        |   | $(0.4132 \times \cos 55)$ |
|        | = | $-0.3294$ |

| Fix Lat | = | $55 + 0.0513$ |
|---------|---|----------------|
|         | = | $55°.0513$ convert to degrees and minutes |
|         | = | $55° \, 03'$ |
| Fix Long | = | $5 + (-0.3294)$ |
|          | = | $4°.6706$ convert to degrees and minutes |
|          | = | $4° \, 40'$ |

*Fix   =   55° 03' N 04° 40' E*

This fix was obtained from two sextant sights: Vega and Alde-baran. Obviously, the more sights taken, the more accurate the fix. In this respect astro-navigation is identical to coastal navigation, where the intersection of three position lines from three different bearings gives the navigator much more confidence in his fix than one from only two bearings. However, this is not always possible, especially in astro-navigation where the only heavenly body visible all day is the sun. In this case, the astro-navigator does the same as a coastal navigator who has only one object from which a bearing is obtainable; he uses a running fix to determine his position. This will be the subject of the next chapter.

Returning to the example in this chapter; stars, planets and the moon offer the best chance of obtaining the most accurate fix from multiple sights, as they are all visible together. Unfortunately, how-ever, there is only a limited time in which to obtain such sights. A sextant sight requires the horizon to be visible as well as a heavenly body. The only times when it will be light enough to see the horizon, yet dark enough to see the stars, planets and moon, are dawn and dusk. At these times multiple twilight sights are possible and a really accurate fix can be obtained. In daylight it is sometimes possible to get a moon or planet sight as well as the sun. Whichever bodies are sighted, the *exact* time of each sight must be recorded, even if the yacht is not making way or is travelling at such a speed that there is no practical change of EP between sights.

When three or more sights are plotted by traditional methods it is immediately apparent if the fix is reliable. An unreliable fix is dis-closed by a large 'cocked hat' at the intersection of the position lines and indicates that one or more of the azimuths or intercepts is inaccurate. By calculator no such visual check is possible, but the RGO tables do include a calculator formula for predicting the size of a cocked hat statistically. Nevertheless, if any doubts remain about the reliability of a calculator fix, it can always be checked by plotting three or more position lines on graph paper. Unfortunately, the accuracy of a fix from only two sights, whether by calculator or plotting, cannot be checked visually or statistically. Conversely, however, a calculator fix can be used to check a traditional fix where the cocked hat is not so large as to warrant discarding the fix, but large enough to be doubtful. All the examples and exercises in this book can be checked by traditional methods and it makes an interesting and worthwhile exercise to do so.

*Example*
At dusk on 31 December 1981 at EP 49°N 02°W, the following star sights were obtained:

at 1640 GMT Capella 32° 25.4′;
at 1642 Diphda 19° 41′;
at 1643 Vega 40° 51.5′.
Calculate the yacht's position.

$GHA\gamma$ = $A + 0.985647x + 15\ GMT$
RGO tables, see Appendix B: $A = 68.7810$   $x = 31 + GMT/24$

|  | *Capella* | *Diphda* | *Vega* |
|---|---|---|---|
| GMT | 16.6667 | 16.7000 | 16.7167 |
| **GHA$\gamma$** | 350.0205 | 350.5219 | 350.7726 |

$\begin{matrix} SHA \\ Dec \end{matrix}$ = $a_0 + 0.0001\ (a_1 + a_2x)$

RGO tables, see Appendix B

| SHA $a_0$ | 281.1561 | 349.3260 | 80.9136 |
|---|---|---|---|
| $a_1$ | 0 | 9 | 99 |
| $a_2$ | −0.5 | 0.6 | 0.1 |
| **SHA** | 281.1545 | 349.3288 | 80.9238 |

| Dec $a_0$ | 45.9771 | S 18.0859 | 38.7617 |
|---|---|---|---|
| $a_1$ | 23 | 25 | 78 |
| $a_2$ | 0.4 | 0.3 | −0.8 |
| **Dec** | 45.9807 | −18.0894 | 38.7670 |

LHA* = $GHA\gamma + SHA + EP\ Long$
**LHA*** | 269.1750 | 337.8507 | 69.6964 |

sin Hc = $sin\ Lat\ sin\ Dec + cos\ Lat\ cos\ Dec\ cos\ LHA$
= 0.5362 | 0.3433 | 0.6501 |

|            | *Capella* | *Diphda* | *Vega*   |
|------------|-----------|----------|----------|
| **Hc**     | 32.4221   | 20.0765  | 40.5463  |

Az   =   R→P   x and y
x    =   cos Lat sin Dec − sin Lat cos Dec cos LHA

|   | = | 0.4793 | −0.8682 | 0.2066 |
|---|---|--------|---------|--------|

y    =   −cos Dec sin LHA

|         | = | 0.6948  | 0.3584   | −0.7313   |
|---------|---|---------|----------|-----------|
| **Az**  |   | 55.4002 | 157.5688 | 285.7755  |

|        |   | 32.4233 | 19.6833  | 40.8583 |
|--------|---|---------|----------|---------|
| Ho     |   |         |          |         |

p    =   Ho − Hc

|        |   | 0.0012 | −0.3932 | 0.3120 |
|--------|---|--------|---------|--------|
| **p**  |   |        |         |        |

| A | = | $\cos^2$ Az     | (Capella + Diphda + Vega) |
|---|---|-----------------|---------------------------|
| B | = | cos Az sin Az   | (Capella + Diphda + Vega) |
| C | = | $\sin^2$ Az     | (Capella + Diphda + Vega) |
| D | = | p cos Az        | (Capella + Diphda + Vega) |
| E | = | p sin Az        | (Capella + Diphda + Vega) |

| A | = | 0.3224 + 0.8544 + 0.0739      |
|---|---|-------------------------------|
|   | = | 1.2507 (memory 1)             |
| B | = | 0.4674 + −0.3527 + −0.2616    |
|   | = | −0.1469 (memory 2)            |
| C | = | 0.6776 + 0.1456 + 0.9261      |
|   | = | 1.7493 (memory 3)             |

Check A + C  =   3

| G | = | $AC - B^2$          |
|---|---|---------------------|
|   | = | 2.1663 (memory 6)   |
| D | = | 0.0007 + 0.3634 + 0.0848 |
|   | = | 0.4489 (memory 4)   |
| E | = | 0.0010 + −0.1500 + −0.3002 |
|   | = | −0.4492 (memory 5)  |

d.Lat   =   (DC − EB)/G
           =   (memory 4 × memory 3 − memory 5 × memory 2) ÷ memory 6
           =   0°.3320

d.Long  =   (AE − BD)/(G cos EP Lat)
           =   (memory 1 × memory 5 − memory 2 × memory 4) ÷ (memory 6 × cos 49)
           =   −0°.3489

Fix Lat   =   49 + 0.3320
          =   49°.3320

Fix Long $= -2 + -0.3489$
$\qquad\qquad = -2°.3489$

*Fix $= 49° 20'N 2° 21'W$*

By now, if not before, it will have become apparent how useful it is to possess a calculator with several memories. The minimum is three, but the more there are the quicker the final result appears. However, if your calculator does have insufficient memory capacity, just write down the intermediate results on paper instead of using the calculator memory.

**Summary**

Fix $=$ EP Lat $+$ d.Lat
$\qquad\quad$ EP Long $+$ d.Long

d.Lat $=$ $(DC-EB)/G$
d.Long $=$ $(AE-BD)/(G \cos EP \, Lat)$

A $=$ total of $\cos^2 Az$ for each sight
B $=$ total of $\cos Az \sin Az$ for each sight
C $=$ total of $\sin^2 Az$ for each sight
D $=$ total of $p \cos Az$ for each sight
E $=$ total of $p \sin Az$ for each sight

Check A $+$ C $=$ number of sights
G $=$ $AC-B^2$
p $=$ $Ho-Hc$
Az $=$ calculated bearing of sight

**Exercise 5** (Answers in Appendix C)

1 At EP 4° 09′S 45° 31′E the following intercepts and azimuths were obtained from star sights:
Altair $\quad$ 0°.1543, 080°
Arcturus $\quad$ 0°.0987, 335°
Fix the ship's position.
2 At EP 36° 42′N 08° 55′W the following intercepts and azimuths were obtained from star sights:
Vega $\qquad$ 0°.0421, 068°
Spica $\qquad$ 0°.0096, 202°
Dubhe $\quad$ −0°.0786, 325°
Fix the yacht's position
3 At EP 55° 48′N 08° 59′W on 1 December 1981, the sextant altitude of Venus was 9° 43′ at 15h01m38s. At 15h03m05s GMT the sextant altitude of the sun was 5° 19′. Fix the ship's position.

4 At EP 35° 17'N 18° 02'W on 1 September 1981, at 21h30m06s GMT, the sextant altitude of Antares was 18° 01'. At 21h32m14s the sextant altitude of Altair was 61° 27'. Fix the yacht's position.

5 At EP 55° 31'N 08° 34'W on 1 December 1981, the following sextant altitudes were recorded:
16h30m04s GMT Alpheratz 44° 39'
1632 GMT Vega 63° 13'
16h33m58s GMT Alioth 32° 50'
Fix the yacht's position.

# 8

# Running Fix

The previous chapter showed how to calculate a fix when two or more sights are taken from the same position. This necessitates the presence of two or more different heavenly bodies of which sights can be taken. By day, there is usually only one body visible (the sun) and a position cannot be fixed from only one sight. The astronavigator accordingly follows the technique used by coastal navigators faced with the same problem of only one object from which a bearing can be taken. They fix their position by means of a **running fix**.

For a running fix, a bearing is taken of the single object available. This is recorded, together with the time, log reading and course steered. A second bearing is taken later and the same data recorded. The navigator now has two bearings and knows the course steered and distance travelled between them. The traditional chartwork method of fixing position is to draw the first bearing ($PL_1$) on the chart and mark on it the estimated position ($EP_1$). From $EP_1$ the course made good and distance made good between the two bearings are then marked. This gives the estimated position ($EP_2$) at which the second bearing was taken. The second bearing ($PL_2$) is then drawn on the chart (Fig 14).

The first bearing is now transferred to $EP_2$ by drawing it through $EP_2$ parallel to $PL_1$ (Fig 15). The intersection of the transferred

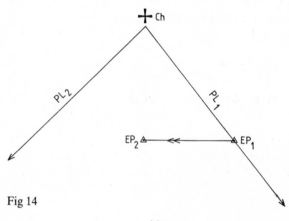

Fig 14

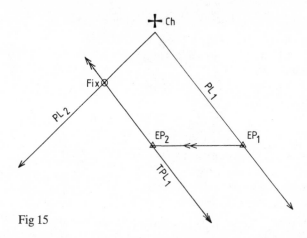

Fig 15

position line (TPL$_1$) with the second bearing PL$_2$ gives the fix. In this example both bearings were taken of the same object, but in practice the second bearing may be taken from a different one.

It is apparent from Fig 15 that if EP$_1$ and EP$_2$ are known, there is no need to draw the first bearing PL$_1$ on the chart. It is only necessary to draw it as a transferred position line through EP$_2$, whereupon its intersection with PL$_2$ provides a fix. So we are now back to the situation described in the previous chapter where we have an estimated position and two bearings, ie EP$_2$ and position lines TPL$_1$ and PL$_2$. These position lines are in the form of an intercept and azimuth and calculation of the fix is performed as follows:

1  First sextant sight from EP$_1$.
2  Calculate intercept (p$_1$) and azimuth (Az$_1$).
3  Second sextant sight from EP$_2$.
4  Calculate EP$_2$.
5  Calculate intercept (p$_2$) and azimuth (Az$_2$).
6  Calculate d.Lat and d.Long as if both sights were taken from EP$_2$.
7  Fix  =  EP$_2$ Lat  + d.Lat
          EP$_2$ Long + d.Long

If a third sight is taken, the fix is calculated from EP$_3$.

*Example*
1  At EP 51° 30′N 01° 30′E a sun sight gave an intercept of 0°.0333 and azimuth 098°. The yacht then made good a course and distance of 060° 25 miles; when another sun sight gave an intercept of −0°.0833 and azimuth 169°. Calculate the yacht's position at the time of the second sight.

45

To find $EP_2$ refer back to Chapter 3 if necessary.

$EP_2$ = $EP_1$ + d.Lat, d.Long
d.Lat, d.Long = P→R 25M 060°
By calculator:
d.Lat = 12.5'
departure = 21.6506M
d.Long' = departure/cos mean Lat
= 21.6506 ÷ cos 51.6042
= 34.8590'
$EP_2$ Lat = 51° 30' + 12.5'
= 51°.7083
$EP_2$ Long = 01° 30' + 34.8590'
= 02°.0810

$Az_1 = 098°$ $Az_2 = 169°$ $p_1 = 0°.0333$ $p_2 = -0°.0833$

A = $\cos^2 Az_1 + \cos^2 Az_2$
= 0.9830
B = $\cos Az_1 \sin Az_1 + \cos Az_2 \sin Az_2$
= −0.3251
C = $\sin^2 Az_1 + \sin^2 Az_2$
= 1.0170
Check A + C = 2
G = $AC - B^2$
= 0.8940
D = $p_1 \cos Az_1 + p_2 \cos Az_2$
= 0.0771
E = $p_1 \sin Az_1 + p_2 \sin Az_2$
= 0.0171

d.Lat = (DC−EB)/G
= 0.0939
d.Long = (AE−BD)/(G cos $EP_2$ Lat)
= 0.0756

Fix = $EP_2$ Lat + d.Lat
$EP_2$ Long + d.Long
= 51.7083 + 0.0939 = 51°.8022
2.0810 + 0.0756 = 2°.1566
= *51° 48' N 02° 09.4' E*

2 At EP 39°N 09° 30'E on 4 December 1981, at 09h16m30s GMT,
the sextant altitude of the sun was 22° 56.5'. The yacht then made
good a course and distance of 130° 28 miles, when at 13h20m15s
GMT another sun sight gave an altitude of 21° 49'. Find the yacht's
position when the second sight was taken.

$EP_1 \rightarrow EP_2$
$$\left.\begin{array}{l} \text{d.Lat} \\ \text{departure} \end{array}\right\} = \text{P} \rightarrow \text{R} \quad 130° \quad 28\text{M}$$

d.Lat   =   $-17.9981'$
dep     =   21.4492M
d.Long  =   27.5417'

|              | 1st sight   | 2nd sight   |
|--------------|-------------|-------------|
| GMT          | 9.2750      | 13.3375     |
| EP Lat       | 39.0        | 38.70       |
| EP Long      | 9.50        | 9.9590      |
| Ho           | 22.9417     | 21.8167     |

RGO tables, see Appendix B

|     | 1st sight | 2nd sight |
|-----|-----------|-----------|
| GHA | 321.5748  | 22.4952   |
| Dec | $-22.2490$ | $-22.2715$ |
| LHA | 331.0748  | 32.4542   |

$\sin \text{Hc}$ = $\sin \text{Lat} \sin \text{Dec} + \cos \text{Lat} \cos \text{Dec} \cos \text{LHA}$
$\quad$ Az = $\text{R} \rightarrow \text{P} \quad x\, y$
$\quad$ x = $\cos \text{Lat} \sin \text{Dec} - \sin \text{Lat} \cos \text{Dec} \cos \text{LHA}$
$\quad$ y = $-\cos \text{Dec} \sin \text{LHA}$
$\quad$ p = $\text{Ho} - \text{Hc}$

| Hc | 23.0338   | 21.8668   |
| p  | $-0.0921$ | $-0.0501$ |
| Az | 150.8932  | 212.3501  |

A  =  1.4771$\quad\quad$B  =  0.0270$\quad$C  =  0.5229
$\quad\quad\quad$Check A + C  =  2
G  =  0.7716$\quad\quad\quad$D  =  0.1230$\quad$E  =  $-0.0180$

d.Lat$\quad\quad$ = $\quad (\text{DC} - \text{EB})/\text{G}$
$\quad\quad\quad\quad\quad$ = $\quad 0.0840$
Fix Lat$\quad\quad$ = $\quad EP_2 \text{Lat} + \text{d.Lat}$
$\quad\quad\quad\quad\quad$ = $\quad 38°.7840$
d.Long$\quad\quad$ = $\quad (\text{AE} - \text{BD})/(\text{G} \cos EP_2 \text{Lat})$
$\quad\quad\quad\quad\quad$ = $\quad -0.0496$
Fix Long$\quad$ = $\quad EP_2 \text{Long} + \text{d.Long}$
$\quad\quad\quad\quad\quad$ = $\quad 09°.9094$

*Fix  =  38° 47' N 09° 54.6' E*

**Summary**

Position by Running Fix
1 Take a sextant sight at $EP_1$
2 Calculate intercept $p_1$ and azimuth $Az_1$
3 Take sextant sight at $EP_2$
4 Calculate $EP_2$
5 Calculate intercept $p_2$ and azimuth $Az_2$
6 Calculate d.Lat and d.Long from $EP_2$
7 Fix = $EP_2$ Lat + d.Lat
$EP_2$ Long + d.Long

**Exercise 6** (Answers in Appendix C)

1 A sextant sight from a yacht at EP 41° 10′N 2° 31′E gave an azimuth and intercept of 120°, 0°.2015. The yacht then made good a course and distance of 200°, 50 miles, when a further sextant sight gave an azimuth and intercept of 210°, −0°.1762. Fix the yacht's position.
2 A yacht in position 0° 16′S 0° 09′E made good a course and distance of 320°, 40 miles. A sextant sight then gave an azimuth and intercept of 100°, −0°.1632. The yacht then made good a course and distance of 341°, 25 miles, when another sight gave an azimuth and intercept of 150°, 0°.2007. Fix the yacht's position.
3 On 4 October 1981 at EP 35° 57′N 01° 05′E, a sun sight at 9h16m25s GMT gave an altitude of 37° 01′. The yacht then made good a course and distance of 070°, 30 miles, when at 15h00m45s GMT a sun sight gave an altitude of 28° 05′. Fix the yacht's position.
4 On 26 December 1981 at EP 50° 02′N 6°W, a sextant sight of Venus at 15h10m49s GMT gave an altitude of 21° 50′. The yacht then made good a course of 330° for 20 miles, when at 1730 GMT a sextant sight of Altair gave an altitude of 29° 32′. Fix the yacht's position.
5 On 1 October 1981 at EP 30°N 15°W, a sextant sight of the moon at 17h05m22s GMT gave an altitude of 40° 57′. The yacht then made good a course and distance of 120°, 74 miles, when at 06h21m45s GMT, the next day, a sextant sight of Regulus gave an altitude of 32° 09′. Fix the yacht's position.

# 9

# Latitude by Meridian Altitude

To observers on Earth, heavenly bodies rise in the east and move westwards; gradually increasing their altitude until they are due south (or north) of the observer. At this point of maximum altitude they are on the same meridian as the observer; and the *local* time (not GMT) at which this occurs is called the time of meridian passage. After this time the body continues moving westwards with a gradually decreasing altitude until it sets in the west.

In the case of the sun the time of meridian passage is local noon but it may be at any time for the moon, planets and stars. If a body is observed by sextant just before its meridian passage it will be necessary to increase the sextant angle gradually as it continues to rise; whereupon, at the exact time of meridian passage, it will stop rising; and no further increase in sextant angle will be required to keep it on the horizon. A little while later it will appear to sink below the horizon and no more sextant adjustments should be made. The time (GMT) at which the body reached its maximum altitude is recorded, together with the maximum sextant altitude. The true latitude of the observer at the time of meridian passage is given by the formula:

$$\text{Latitude} = 90 + \text{Alt} + \text{Dec} \quad (-180)$$

where Alt is the maximum sextant altitude and Dec is the declination of the body at the time of meridian passage. The derivation of this formula is explained in the following diagrams. Fig 16 shows an observer at Z and his horizon HZH. The point directly overhead of

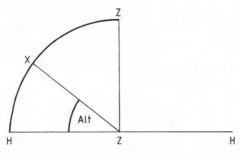

Fig 16

the observer is called the observer's zenith (also called Z). Obviously the angle ZZH between the observer's horizon and his zenith is a right angle and is represented by arc ZH.

If the observer at Z takes a sextant altitude of a heavenly body X at the time of meridian passage, then arc ZXH is the observer's meridian. The altitude of the body, angle HZX, equals arc HX, whilst arc XZ equals 90° minus altitude. In other words 90° minus altitude equals the angular difference between the position of the heavenly body X and the observer's zenith Z.

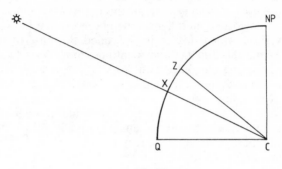

Fig 17

Fig 17 shows the same situation in relation to the equator Q, centre of the earth C and north pole NP. The geographical position of the body and observer's zenith are again X and Z. From this diagram the observer's latitude is arc QZ. But QZ = QX + XZ. QX is the body's declination and (as shown in Fig 16) XZ = 90° − altitude. So the observer's latitude QZ equals: declination + (90° − altitude).

In this example, in the northern hemisphere in summer, if the observer's latitude is 50°N and the sun's declination is 20°N, we would have:

$$QZ = 50 \qquad QX = 20 \qquad XZ = 30$$

But XZ = 90° − altitude; so the altitude of the sun in this example would be 60°. Furthermore the observer would see the sun bearing due south at the time of meridian passage. By the calculator rule of naming southerly bearings negative, the altitude is entered as −60. Hence the calculator formula:

$$\text{Latitude} = 90 + \text{Alt} + \text{Dec} \quad (-180)$$

In this case the latitude (50) equals:

$$90 + (-60) + 20$$

50

Fig 18 shows a similar situation with declination still 20°N but observer's latitude 12°N.

$$QZ = 12 \qquad QX = 20 \qquad XZ = 8 = 90° - \text{altitude}$$

The sun's altitude in this case would be 82° bearing north of the observer. By the calculator formula we have:

$$
\begin{aligned}
\text{Latitude (12)} \quad &= \quad 90 + \text{Alt} + \text{Dec} \quad (-180) \\
&= \quad 90 + 82 + 20 \\
&= \quad 192
\end{aligned}
$$

By definition, latitude cannot be greater than 90°. Hence the bracket $(-180)$ at the end of the formula. If the answer is greater than 90, subtract 180 to give the correct latitude. In this case 192 — 180 = 12. Thus the latitude is 12°N.

Fig 19 gives an example of a winter observation with observer Z at latitude 50°N but the sun's declination is now 15°S.

$$QZ = 50 \qquad QX = 15 \qquad XZ = 65 = 90 - \text{altitude}$$

Hence the sun's altitude would be 25° bearing south.

$$
\begin{aligned}
\text{Latitude} \quad &= \quad 90 + \text{Alt} + \text{Dec} \quad (-180) \\
&= \quad 90 + (-25) + (-15) \\
&= \quad \mathit{50°N}
\end{aligned}
$$

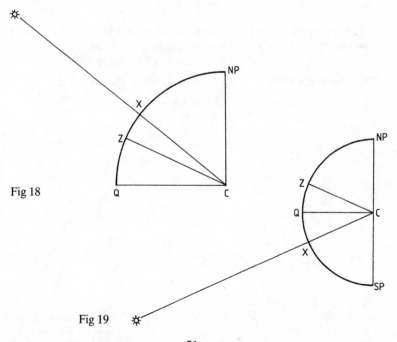

Fig 18

Fig 19

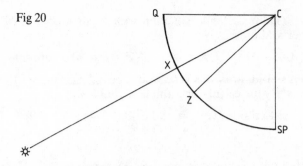

Fig 20

Fig 20 shows an observer in the southern hemisphere. Here the observer is at latitude 50°S and the sun's declination is 20°S. We then have:

$$QZ = 50 \qquad QX = 20 \qquad XZ = 30 = 90 - \text{altitude}$$

Hence the sun's altitude would be 60° bearing north of the observer.

$$
\begin{aligned}
\text{Latitude} &= 90 + \text{Alt} + \text{Dec} \quad (-180) \\
&= 90 + 60 + (-20) \\
&= 130 \quad (-180) \\
&= -50 \\
&= \textit{50°S}
\end{aligned}
$$

The next possible set of circumstances is shown in Fig 21 with an observer in latitude 50°S. The sun's declination is 20°N.

$$QZ = 50 \qquad QX = 20 \qquad XZ = 70 = 90 - \text{altitude}$$

Thus the sun's altitude is 20° bearing north of the observer.

$$
\begin{aligned}
\text{Latitude} &= 90 + \text{Alt} + \text{Dec} \quad (-180) \\
&= 90 + 20 + 20 \\
&= 130 \quad (-180) \\
&= -50 \\
&= \textit{50°S}
\end{aligned}
$$

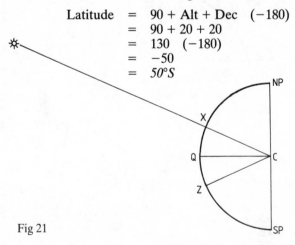

Fig 21

The final diagram (Fig 22) shows an observer in latitude 12°S. Sun's declination is 20°S.

$$QZ = 12 \qquad QX = 20 \qquad XZ = 8 = 90 - \text{altitude}.$$

Altitude is accordingly 82° bearing south.

$$
\begin{aligned}
\text{Latitude} \quad &= \quad 90 + \text{Alt} + \text{Dec} \quad (-180) \\
&= \quad 90 + (-82) + (-20) \\
&= \quad -12 \\
&= \quad 12°S
\end{aligned}
$$

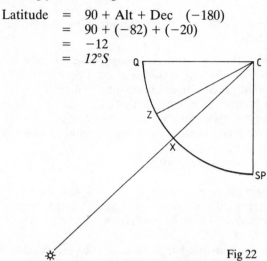

Fig 22

*Examples*

1  Sun's meridian altitude 80°S, declination 20°S.
$$
\begin{aligned}
\text{Latitude} \quad &= \quad 90 + (-80) + (-20) \\
&= \quad -10 \\
&= \quad 10°S
\end{aligned}
$$

2  Meridian altitude 22°S, declination 23°S.
$$
\begin{aligned}
\text{Latitude} \quad &= \quad 90 + (-22) + (-23) \\
&= \quad 45 \\
&= \quad 45°N
\end{aligned}
$$

3  Meridian altitude 49°N, declination 1°S.
$$
\begin{aligned}
\text{Latitude} \quad &= \quad 90 + 49 + (-1) \\
&= \quad 138 \quad (-180) \\
&= \quad -42 \\
&= \quad 42°S
\end{aligned}
$$

4  Meridian altitude 52°S, declination 19°N.
$$
\begin{aligned}
\text{Latitude} \quad &= \quad 90 + (-52) + 19 \\
&= \quad 57 \\
&= \quad 57°N
\end{aligned}
$$

53

5 Meridian altitude 36°N, declination 15°N.

Latitude = 90 + 36 + 15
= 141  (−180)
= −39
= *39°S*

In practice the procedure for obtaining true latitude by meridian altitude is:

1 Find time of meridian passage. This is local noon for sun sights but can be any time for other heavenly bodies. Chapter 11 discusses how to calculate time of meridian passage.
2 Record sextant meridian altitude and time. Time means GMT by the navigator's watch, not local time.
3 Use RGO tables to calculate declination of body at GMT of meridian passage.
4 Calculate true latitude.

Determining true latitude in this simple way gives a single position line. Intercept p equals the difference between the true and EP latitudes. It may be positive or negative but the azimuth Az is always 360°.

Having converted true latitude into terms of an intercept and azimuth, a fix can be calculated if another sextant sight is, or has been, taken. In the case of the sun it is common practice to fix position by running fix from a morning sight to a noon sight; and then by running fix from the noon sight to an afternoon sun sight or twilight star sight. Better still, if two bodies are visible, the altitude of one can be taken immediately after the meridian sight of the other.

*Examples*
1 On 10 December 1981 at EP 50° 05′N 0° 06′W, at 14h58m38s GMT, the meridian altitude of Venus was 18° 01.25′ bearing south. Immediately afterwards at 15h01m15s GMT a sun sight gave an altitude of 5° 59.7′. Find the yacht's position.

The procedure for solving this problem is:

1 Calculate declination of Venus for time of meridian passage.
Declination = −21°.9791
2 Calculate true latitude.
90 + Alt + Dec = 50°.0001  (50°N)
3 Calculate intercept p.
p = true Lat − EP Lat
= 50.0001 − 50.0833
= −0.0832

4 Azimuth is 360°.
5 Calculate GHA, declination and LHA for second sight.
6 Calculate Hc and Az for second sight.

sin Hc = sin EP Lat sin Dec + cos EP Lat cos Dec cos LHA

Az = polar co-ordinate angle of rectangular co-ordinates x and y.

x = cos EP Lat sin Dec − sin EP Lat cos Dec cos LHA

y = −cos Dec sin LHA

7 Calculate p = Ho − Hc
8 Calculate values A to E and G.

A = $\cos^2 Az_1 + \cos^2 Az_2$

B = $\cos Az_1 \sin Az_1 + \cos Az_2 \sin Az_2$

C = $\sin^2 Az_1 + \sin^2 Az_2$

Check A + C = number of sights (2)

G = $AC - B^2$

D = $p_1 \cos Az_1 + p_2 \cos Az_2$

E = $p_1 \sin Az_1 + p_2 \sin Az_2$

9 Calculate d.Long = (AE − BD)/(G cos EP Lat)

10 Fix = $\begin{cases} \text{True latitude} \quad (\text{step 2}) \\ \text{EP Long + d.Long} \end{cases}$

|       | *Venus*   | *Sun*    |
|-------|-----------|----------|
| GMT   | 14.9772   | 15.0208  |
| Ho    | −18.0208  | 5.9950   |
| Dec   | −21.9791  | −22.9409 |
| EP Lat | 50.0833  | 50.0833  |
| EP Long |         | −0.1000  |
| GHA   |           | 47.0910  |
| LHA   |           | 46.9910  |
| Hc    |           | 5.9766   |
| Az    | 360.0000  | 222.6167 |
| p     | −0.0832   | 0.0184   |

A = 1.5415  B = 0.4983  C = 0.4585

Check A + C = 2

D = −0.0967  E = −0.0125  G = 0.4585

d.Long = 0°.0983

Fix Long = −0.1000 + 0.0983

= −0°.0017

There is no need to calculate d.Lat as the true latitude was found from the meridian altitude of Venus (step 2).

*Yacht's position 50°N 0° 00.1′W*

In this particular example the sun's altitude was just under 6°. But in practice, altitudes below 10° should be avoided whenever possible as refraction error is greatest at low altitudes. Although such error can be corrected (as shown in Chapter 14), altitudes below 10° should be treated with caution.

2 On 31 December 1981, at EP 33° 23'S 31° 29'E, a sun sight at 07h22m13s GMT gave an altitude of 54° 30.2'. The yacht then made good a course and distance of 140° 14.8 miles when at 09h56m52s GMT the meridian altitude of the sun bearing north was 79° 39.1'. Find the yacht's position.

*1st sight*
From RGO tables (see Appendix B) calculate GHA and declination. Then calculate Hc, Az and p.
*2nd sight*
Calculate $EP_2$ and declination.

$$EP_2 = EP_1 + P{\to}R \text{ course and distance}$$

$$\left.\begin{array}{r} 14.8 \\ 140 \end{array}\right\} \; P{\to}R \; = \; \left\{\begin{array}{lll} \text{d.Lat} & = & -11.3375' & = & -0°.1890 \\ \text{dep} & = & 9.5133M \end{array}\right.$$

$$\begin{aligned} \text{d.Long} & = & \text{dep/cos mean Lat} \\ & = & 11.4504' & = & 0°.1901 \end{aligned}$$

$$\begin{aligned} EP_2 \text{ Lat} & = & -33°.5723 \\ EP_2 \text{ Long} & = & 31°.6734 \end{aligned}$$

$$\begin{aligned} \text{Calculate true latitude} & = & 90 + \text{Alt} + \text{Dec} \quad (-180) \\ & = & -33°.4383 \\ & = & 33° 26.3'S \end{aligned}$$

$$\begin{aligned} \text{Calculate intercept p} & = & \text{true Lat} - \text{EP Lat} \\ & = & -33.4383 - (-33.5723) \\ & = & 0.1340 \end{aligned}$$

$$\text{Azimuth} \; = \; 360°$$

|       | *1st sight* | *2nd sight* |
|-------|-------------|-------------|
| GMT   | 7.3703      | 9.9478      |
| EP Lat | −33.3833   | −33.5723    |
| EP Long | 31.4833   | 31.6734     |
| GHA   | 289.8139    |             |
| LHA   | 321.2972    |             |
| Dec   | −23.0979    | −23.0900    |
| Ho    | 54.5033     | 79.6517     |
| Hc    | 54.6133     |             |
| Az    | 83.3157     | 360.0000    |
| p     | −0.1100     | 0.1340      |

$$A = 1.0135 \quad B = 0.1156 \quad C = 0.9865$$
Check A + C = 2
$$D = 0.1212 \quad E = -0.1093 \quad G = 0.9865$$

d.Long $= (AE - BD)/(G \cos EP_2 \text{ Lat})$
$\quad\quad\quad = -0°.1518$
Fix Long $= EP_2 \text{ Long} + \text{d.Long}$
$\quad\quad\quad = 31°.5216$

*Yacht's position 33° 26.3'S  31° 31.3'E*

**Summary**

True latitude = 90 + meridian altitude + declination   (−180)
Meridian altitude bearing north is positive
Meridian altitude bearing south is negative

p   =   true latitude − EP latitude

Az  =   360°

**Exercise 7** (Answers in Appendix C)

1 Calculate the true latitude from the following meridian altitudes:
   (a) Sun, bearing south, 50°; declination 10°N.
   (b) Sun, bearing south, 34°; declination  5°S.
   (c) Sun, bearing north, 50°; declination 15°N.
   (d) Sun, bearing north, 50°; declination 15°S.
   (e) Sun, bearing south, 84°; declination 18°S.
   (f) Sun, bearing north, 75°; declination 22°N.
2 At 11h55m47s GMT on 20 December 1981, the meridian altitude of the sun was 15° 09' bearing south. What was the yacht's latitude?
3 At EP 52° 58'N 5° 01'W on 17 November 1981, at 06h42m29s GMT, the meridian altitude of Regulus was 49° 04' bearing south. At 06h44m01s GMT the altitude of Capella was 44° 02'. What was the yacht's position?
4 On 6 October 1981 at EP 52° 30'N 4° 04'E, a sextant sight of the sun at 08h02m19s GMT gave an altitude of 17° 36'. The yacht then made good a course and distance of 230° 40M, when at 18h04m09s GMT the meridian altitude of the moon was 16° 38' bearing south. Fix the yacht's position.
5 At 14h36m05s GMT on 20 December 1981, at EP 51° 29'N 0° 46'E, the meridian altitude of Venus was 19° 08' bearing south. The yacht then sailed 060° for 15 miles, when at 1700 GMT the altitude of Vega was 43° 22'. Fix the yacht's position.

# 10

# Latitude by Pole Star

A simple way of finding latitude was described in the last chapter. It entails a sextant sight of any heavenly body as it passes the observer's meridian. A similar method can be applied to one particular heavenly body, the Pole Star (Polaris).

Polaris is situated directly above the North Pole. It may therefore be said that the North Pole is the geographical position of Polaris and its azimuth is 360°. Unfortunately this is not quite true as Polaris is not, in fact, exactly overhead all the time. The true path of Polaris is a tiny circle directly above the North Pole. However, let us assume for the moment that Polaris is exactly overhead and the North Pole is its GP. Fig 23 shows an observer at Z and his horizon

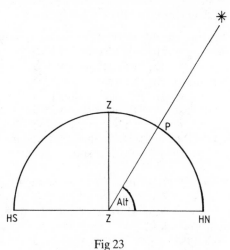

Fig 23

HS Z HN. HS is the southern aspect of his horizon and HN is the northern. His own zenith is Z. If this observer takes a sextant altitude of Polaris (P), then the altitude PZHN is represented by arc PHN and arc PZ equals 90° − altitude. If the equator Q is now inserted into the diagram, Fig 24, we have:

Arc QZ = observer's latitude
Arc PZ = 90 − latitude

58

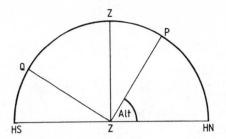

Fig 24

But we have just seen from Fig 23 that arc PZ also equals 90 − altitude of Polaris. Therefore:

90 − altitude  =  90 − latitude
Altitude  =  Latitude

Thus the altitude of Polaris equals the observer's latitude. Unfortunately this only applies if Polaris is *exactly* vertically above the North Pole, whereas in fact Polaris actually describes a small circle around it. To find latitude by Polaris, some corrections have to be applied to the altitude to allow for the fact that Polaris is not exactly overhead at the Pole.

The formulae for latitude by Polaris are:

Latitude  =  $Ho − C + 0.0087 S^2 \tan Ho$
Azimuth  =  $−S / \cos Ho$

where Ho is the true sextant altitude

$C = p \cos LHA \qquad S = p \sin LHA$

It is important to note at this stage that p is not the same value as intercept p which we have used before where $p = Ho − Hc$. In this case, and this case only, p means the polar distance, ie the distance of the GP of Polaris from the North Pole.

LHA Polaris  =  GHA Aries + SHA Polaris + EP Longitude

GHA Aries, SHA Polaris and p are all found from the RGO tables.

GHA Aries (GHA$\gamma$)  =  $A + 0.985647x + 15$ GMT
SHA Polaris  =  $70 (a_0 + 0.0001 (a_1 + a_2x))$
Polar Distance p  =  $a_0 + 0.0001 (a_1 + a_2x)$

In all these formulae:  $x = $ date + GMT/24

*Examples*
1 Find the SHA and polar distance of Polaris on 22 September 1981 at 1845 GMT at EP 52°N 3°E.

59

*SHA*
RGO tables, see Appendix B
$a_0$     =    4.6610
$a_1$     =    29
$a_2$     =    −0.6
x        =    22 + 18.75 ÷ 24
         =    22.7813
SHA      =    70 (4.6610 + 0.0001 (29 + (−0.6 × 22.7813)))
         =    *326.3773*

*p*
RGO tables, see Appendix B
$a_0$     =    0.8165
$a_1$     =    86
$a_2$     =    −0.8

p        =    0.8165 + 0.0001 (86 + −0.8 × 22.7813)
         =    *0.8233*

2 If, in the previous example, the sextant altitude of Polaris was
51° 45′ find the yacht's latitude.

We have already calculated:
SHA              =    326.3773
Polar distance   =       0.8233
We now have to calculate
LHA Polaris      =    GHAγ + SHA + EP Long
RGO tables, see Appendix B
GHAγ     =    339.0871 + 0.985647 × 22.7813 + 15 × 18.75
         =    642.7914   (−360)
         =    282.7914

LHA*     =    282.7914 + 326.3773 + 3
         =    612.1687   (−360)
         =    252.1687

C        =    p cos LHA
         =       0.8233 × cos 252.1687
         =    −0.2521

S        =    p sin LHA
         =    −0.7837

Lat      =    Ho − C + 0.0087 S$^2$ tan Ho
         =    51.75 − (−0.2521) + 0.0087 × (−0.7837)$^2$ × tan 51.75
         =    *52°.0089*

Az       =    −S/cos Ho
         =    −(−0.7837) ÷ cos 51.75
         =    *1°.2659*

Latitude by Polaris differs from latitude by meridian altitude insofar as it requires the value of LHA; and this depends on an estimated longitude. Thus the latitude and azimuth obtained are really approximations. Furthermore, unless the azimuth is exactly 360°, the position line is not a true parallel of latitude. For practical purposes, however, the latitude is sufficiently accurate to be regarded as a true value, and the calculation of azimuth can be skipped. The latter does not vary from 360° by more than 3° and may conveniently be regarded as 360°.

In the following example and exercise d.Lat and true Lat are actually calculated for the sake of it from A to G values; and the calculated azimuth is used as well. But in practice there is no need to use them; just find true latitude from the Polaris formula and use 360° for the azimuth.

3 Immediately after the Polaris sight, at 1847 GMT, the sextant altitude of Arcturus was 25° 37.5′. Find the yacht's position.

The first step in solving this problem is to calculate the *intercept* p for Polaris. This equals the difference between the true and EP latitudes. It may be positive or negative.

$$\text{Intercept p} \quad = \quad \text{true latitude} - \text{EP latitude}$$
$$= \quad 52.0089 - 52$$
$$= \quad 0°.0089$$

The next step is to calculate GHAγ, SHA, LHA* and declination of Arcturus for the time of observation.

$$\text{LHA* Arcturus} \quad = \quad \text{GHAγ} + \text{SHA} + \text{EP Long}$$

GHAγ, SHA and declination are found from RGO tables (Appendix B).

Next calculate Hc and Az in the usual way and obtain intercept p from Ho − Hc.

Then calculate values A to G.

$$\text{Finally find d.Long} \quad = \quad (AE - BD)/(G \cos \text{EP Lat})$$

There is no need to calculate d.Lat as latitude is already known from the Polaris sight.

|  | *Polaris* | *Arcturus* |
|---|---|---|
| GMT |  | 18.7833 |
| EP Lat | 52.0 | 52.0 |
| EP Long | 3.0 | 3.0 |
| True Lat | 52.0089 |  |
| Ho |  | 25.6250 |
| GHAγ |  | 283.2927 |
| SHA |  | 146.2979 |
| Dec |  | 19.2821 |
| LHA |  | 72.5906 |
| Hc |  | 25.7273 |
| p | 0.0089 | −0.1023 |
| Az | 1.2659 | 268.7762 |

A = 1.0    B = 0.0434    C = 1.0
Check A + C = 2
G = 0.9981    D = 0.0112    E = 0.1025

d.Lat  = 0°.0066
d.Long = 0°.1660
Lat    = 52 + 0.0066
       = 52°.0066
Long   = 3 + 0.1660
       = 3.1660

*Yacht's position is 52° 00.4′ N  3° 10′ E*

Note that the latitude found directly from the Polaris formula is 52°.0089 whereas by using A to G values and the calculated azimuth the true latitude is found to be 52°.0066 — a difference of no navigational significance as far as yachtsmen are concerned.

## Summary

| | | |
|---|---|---|
| SHA Polaris | = | $70(a_0 + 0.0001(a_1 + a_2 x))$ |
| x | = | date + GMT/24 |
| Polar distance | = | $a_0 + 0.0001(a_1 + a_2 x)$ |
| LHA Polaris | = | GHAγ + SHA + EP Long |
| C | = | p cos LHA |
| S | = | p sin LHA |
| Latitude | = | $Ho - C + 0.0087 S^2 \tan Ho$ |
| Azimuth | = | $-S/\cos Ho$ (Use Az 360° in practice) |
| Intercept p | = | true Lat − EP Lat |

**Exercise 8** (Answers in Appendix C)

1 Find the SHA and polar distance of Polaris at EP 60°N 92°W on 30 June 1981 at 0700 GMT.

2 In the above question, the altitude of Polaris is 59° 30′. Find the true latitude, azimuth and intercept.

3 At EP 40°N 6°E on 6 June 1981, at 1800 GMT, the altitude of Polaris was 39° 47′. Find the true latitude, azimuth and intercept.

4 On 4 April 1981 at EP 30° 57′N 18° 40′W the altitude of Polaris at 1930 GMT was 31° 25′. At 1933 the altitude of Regulus was 45° 08′. Find the yacht's position.

5 At EP 46°N 5°W on 5 November 1981 the altitude of Polaris was 45° 52° at 06h02m48s GMT. The yacht then made good a course and distance of 030° 25M, when at 10h32m12s GMT the altitude of the sun was 24° 48′. Fix the yacht's position.

# 11
# Time

The navigator's watch described in Chapter 1 always keeps the correct time and date at Greenwich in the 24 hour mode. Time at Greenwich is abbreviated to GMT and the date to GD. The local time (LT) kept by the yacht, and shown on the cabin clock, varies according to the longitude of the yacht's position. Local time, which may be regarded as time by the sun, governs timing of the yacht's daily routine, such as meal times and duty rotas.

The Earth completes a full rotation of 360° every 24 hours. This means that it rotates through 15° every hour (360 ÷ 24 = 15). At Greenwich, local time is the same as GMT; but in longitude 15°E local time is one hour later than GMT; and in 15°W local time is one hour earlier than GMT. The formula for calculating time is accordingly:

$$LT = GMT + Long^h$$
$$GMT = LT - Long^h$$

where $Long^h$ means longitude in time, not degrees.

$$Long^h = Longitude/15$$

*Examples*
1 At 1900 LT in longitude 30°E, what is GMT?

$$GMT = LT - Long^h$$
$$Long^h = 30 \div 15$$
$$= 2$$
$$GMT = 19 - 2$$
$$= 1700$$

2 At 1900 LT in longitude 30°W, what is GMT?

$$Long^h = -30 \div 15$$
$$= -2$$
$$GMT = 19 - (-2)$$
$$= 2100$$

3 At 1300 GMT in longitude 22° 30′E what is the local time?

$$\text{Long}^h = 22.5 \div 15$$
$$= 1.5$$
$$\text{LT} = 13 + 1.5$$
$$= 1430$$

4 At 1300 GMT in longitude 22° 30′W what is the local time?

$$\text{Long}^h = -22.5 \div 15$$
$$= -1.5$$
$$\text{LT} = 13 + (-1.5)$$
$$= 1130$$

Times of meridian passage, sunset, sunrise and twilight are given in nautical almanacs. These times are given as LT. At Greenwich, this will of course be GMT; but elsewhere, LT must be converted to GMT. The navigator will then know at what time, by his watch, the event will occur; and will also have to use this GMT for subsequent calculations of GHA and declination etc.

*Examples*
1 LT of meridian passage of the sun is 11h43m37s. What will be the GMT at longitude 27°E?

$$\text{GMT} = \text{LT} - \text{Long}^h$$
$$= 11.7269 - 27 \div 15$$
$$= 9.9269$$
$$= 9h55m37s$$

2 LT of meridian passage of Procyon is 06h59m38s. What will be the GMT at 97°W?

$$\text{GMT} = 6.9939 - (-97) \div 15$$
$$= 13.4606$$
$$= 13h27m38s$$

**Zone Time**

When travelling east or west it is necessary to alter local time according to the longitude reached. This ensures that local time by the cabin clock always keeps 'sun time'. For practical convenience in this respect, an international agreement has divided the globe into 24 time zones. Each zone is a band of longitude 15° wide, centred on Greenwich. Zone 0 extends 7½° east and west of Greenwich. Zone −1 extends 15° east of Zone 0, ie from 7½°E to 22½°E. Similarly Zone +1 is 7½°W to 22½°W. All positive zones are west of Greenwich and all negative zones are east. Local time in each zone is called Zone Time (ZT) and clocks displaying zone time are altered at any convenient time after entering a new zone. Astronomical tables are based on GMT but tide tables are usually based on zone time. It is therefore essential to understand how to convert one to the other.

$$ZT = GMT - Zone$$
$$GMT = ZT + Zone$$

*Examples*

1 At 0900 by the navigator's watch, in Zone $-3$, what would be the time on the cabin clock?

| Navigator's watch | = | GMT |
|---|---|---|
| Cabin clock | = | ZT |
| | = | GMT − Zone |
| | = | 9 − (−3) |
| | = | *1200* |

2 At 0900 GMT in Zone $+3$, what is the zone time?

| ZT | = | 9 − 3 |
|---|---|---|
| | = | *0600* |

3 At 0300 GMT, GD 22 May in Zone $+7$, what would be the zone time?

| ZT | = | GMT − Zone |
|---|---|---|
| | = | 3 − 7 |
| | = | −4   (+24) |
| | = | *2000  21 May* |

4 At 2100 GMT, GD 22 May in Zone $-7$, what would be the zone time?

| ZT | = | 21 − (−7) |
|---|---|---|
| | = | 28   (−24) |
| | = | *0400  23 May* |

## Times of Meridian Passage and Twilight

Chapter 9 showed how latitude could be found by taking a sextant sight of a heavenly body as it crosses the observer's meridian. For the sun, this is noon local time; but for the moon, planets and stars it can be any time. It is accordingly necessary to know the time of meridian passage in advance so that the navigator is ready to take the sight at the correct time; and for the moon, planets and stars to check if a twilight or daylight sight is possible.

Star sights are taken at twilight as this is the only period when the horizon and stars are visible at the same time. It is again necessary to know the time of twilight so that the navigator can be ready in good time to identify stars and take the sights in the limited time available.

Times of sunrise, sunset, twilight and meridian passage can be calculated from the data in RGO tables but it necessitates use of a programmable calculator. It is probably easier for a yachtsman to use *Reed's* instead as all the required information is given on the same page.

## Summary

Local time (LT) means Sun time

$$\text{LT} = \text{GMT} + \text{Long}^h$$
$$\text{GMT} = \text{LT} - \text{Long}^h$$
$$\text{Long}^h = \text{Long}/15$$
$$\text{Zone Time (ZT)} = \text{GMT} - \text{Zone}$$
$$\text{GMT} = \text{ZT} + \text{Zone}$$

**Exercise 9** (Answers in Appendix C)

1 What will be the GMT at 1342 local time at:
   a) 15°E     b) 15°W     c) 38° 27′E     d) 100° 48′W
2 What are the times of high water GMT for a zone time of 1306 in:
   a) Zone GMT     b) Zone −2     c) Zone +6
3 At 2019 by the navigator's watch what would be the local time, on the cabin clock, in:
   a) Zone 0     b) Zone +10     c) Zone −3
4 At 2217 GMT on GD 23 May, what would be the local time and date in:
   a) Zone +5     b) Zone 0     c) Zone −8
5 Local time and date of meridian passage of the moon is 0114 on 15 October. What would be the GMT and GD at:
   a) 118°W     b) 49° 17′E

# 12

# Course and Distance

Passages entailing the use of astro-navigation are generally long-distance. In planning such passages it may often be found that the ports of departure and destination are on different charts, which makes it difficult to plot the course and distance between them. It is a simple matter to calculate the course and distance provided the positions of departure and destination are known.

The shortest distance between two points is a straight line. On Mercator charts such a line represents the course and distance between the two points and is called a **rhumb line**. This would certainly be the shortest distance if the earth were flat; but the earth is spherical and a straight line on a sphere is an arc of a **great circle**. A great circle is one which has its centre at the centre of the earth. Thus the shortest distance between two points on the earth's surface is really an arc of a great circle passing through both points.

In practice, for distances of less than 500 miles, the difference between great circle and rhumb line courses is insignificant. Beyond 500 miles, however, the difference increases significantly as the distances increase. For passages of less than 500 miles, rhumb line courses are generally followed whereas great circle courses are used over longer distances.

## Rhumb Lines

The advantage of a rhumb line course is that it cuts all the meridians on a Mercator chart at the same angle, thus giving a constant course angle between the points of departure and destination. A rhumb line course and distance is shown in Fig 25. If A and B are the ports

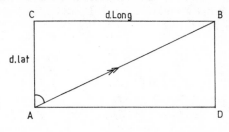

Fig 25

of departure and destination, then angle CAB is the course and AB is the distance. AC is the difference in latitude between A and B (d.Lat); and CB represents the difference in longitude (d.Long). AC and CB are also the rectangular co-ordinates of AB, which is the course and distance from A to B. Conversion of rectangular co-ordinates AC and CB into their polar co-ordinate AB will therefore give the course and distance (refer back to Chapter 3 if necessary). The only snag is that d.Lat AC and d.Long CB must be expressed in the same units. D.Lat in minutes equals nautical miles but d.Long does not. Distance CB in nautical miles is called the departure (dep) and must be calculated as such from the d.Long. The formula for converting d.Long into departure is:

$$\text{Departure} = \text{d.Long (minutes) cos mean Lat}$$

$$\text{Then course and distance AB} = R{\to}P \left\{ \begin{array}{l} \text{d.Lat} \\ \text{d.Long cos mean Lat} \end{array} \right.$$

where mean Lat equals half the sum of latitudes A and B.

*Example*
What is the rhumb line course and distance from Bergen to Aberdeen?

Bergen: 60° 23′N 5° 27′E        Aberdeen: 57° 08′N 2° 04′W

| | | |
|---|---|---|
| d.Lat | = | destination Lat − start Lat |
| | = | 57.1333 − 60.3833 |
| | = | −3°.2500 (negative means course is south) |
| | = | −195 miles |
| d.Long | = | destination Long − start Long |
| | = | −2.0667 − 5.45 |
| | = | −7°.5167 (negative means course is west) |
| mean Lat | = | (60.3833 + 57.1333) ÷ 2 |
| | = | 58°.7583 |
| departure | = | d.Long (minutes) cos mean Lat |
| | = | −7.5167 × 60 × cos 58.7583 |
| | = | −234 miles |
| Course and distance | = | R→P  d.Lat′  departure |
| | = | R→P  −195  −234 |
| | = | 304.5997  −129°.8056  (+360) |
| | = | *305 miles  230°* |

This method of finding the rhumb line distance assumes the earth to be flat and is only valid for short distances. If a required rhumb line distance is more than 500 miles, and an appreciable change of latitude is involved, the curvature of the earth's surface must be taken into account and a different formula used. In Fig 25 the rectangular co-ordinates d.Lat and departure were used to find the rhumb line course and distance; but over longer distances we must use rectangular co-ordinates AC and CB in units of longitude instead of latitude. This is to overcome the distortion of the latitude scale over long distances on a Mercator chart. Thus instead of converting d.Long CB into departure, we convert d.Lat into units of longitude. CB therefore remains as the difference in longitude but distance AC (d.Lat) must be converted into the same units as CB. These units are minutes of longitude but they are converted into **meridional parts** for the latitudes of A and B. A meridional part (M Pt) is the length of a minute of longitude on a Mercator chart and varies according to the latitude. The formula for finding the number of meridional parts for a particular latitude is:

$$\text{M Pts} = 7915.7 \log \tan(45 + 0.5 \, \text{Lat}) - 23.37 \sin \text{Lat}$$

where Lat is the latitude.

These values are found for A and B and then subtracted to give the difference in meridional parts (DMP). Thus:

$$\text{DMP} = \text{M Pts destination} - \text{M Pts start}$$

The rhumb line course is then found by converting d.Long (CB) and DMP (AC) into polar co-ordinates. D.Long is the y co-ordinate and DMP is the x co-ordinate. The resultant polar co-ordinate angle is the true rhumb line course.

Course  =  polar co-ordinate angle of R→P  x and y
x       =  DMP
y       =  d.Long (minutes)

The formula for rhumb line distance is:

$$\text{Distance} = \text{d.Lat/cos course}$$

*Example*
Find the true rhumb line course and distance from Bergen to Aberdeen.
From the previous example we know that:

| d.Lat | = | −195′ |
|---|---|---|
| d.Long | = | −7°.5167 |
| | = | −451′ |
| Aberdeen Lat | = | 57°.1333 |
| Bergen Lat | = | 60°.3833 |

The first step is to find the number of meridional parts for each latitude.

M Pts $\quad=\quad$ 7915.7 log tan(45 + 0.5 Lat) − 23.27 sin Lat

M Pts Aberdeen = 7915.7 log tan(45 + 0.5 × 57.1333)
$\qquad\qquad\qquad$ − 23.27 × sin 57.1333
$\qquad\qquad$ = 4177.7873

M Pts Bergen $\quad=$ 7915.7 log tan(45 + 0.5 × 60.3833)
$\qquad\qquad\qquad$ − 23.27 × sin 60.3833
$\qquad\qquad$ = 4553.4043

Now find the difference in meridional parts.

| DMP | = | M Pts destination − M Pts start |
|---|---|---|
| | = | 4177.7873 − 4553.4043 |
| | = | −375.6170 |

Course $\quad=\quad$ polar co-ordinate angle of R→P x and y
where x $\quad=\quad$ DMP and y = d.Long

| Course | = | R→P −375.6170 −451 |
|---|---|---|
| | = | −129°.7893 (+360) |
| | = | 230°.2107 |

| Distance | = | d.Lat′/cos course |
|---|---|---|
| | = | −195 ÷ cos 230.2107 |
| | = | 304.7033 |

Thus the true rhumb line course and distance from Bergen to Aberdeen is *230° 305 miles*.

For all practical purposes this result is the same as the previous example where the earth was assumed to be flat. This shows that for distances of less than 500 miles we may assume the earth to be flat and use the simpler previous method of calculation; but over longer distances the curvature of the earth's surface is significant and formulae for the true rhumb line course and distance must be used.

### Great Circles

The shortest distance between two points on the earth's surface is an arc of a great circle. On Mercator charts a rhumb line course is a straight line but a great circle course is curved. The reason for this is that Mercator meridians are parallel whereas, in reality, they converge towards the poles. Thus a great circle course on a Mercator chart cuts all the meridians at different angles and a single course to steer is unobtainable. A great circle course must gradually be changed throughout the passage. Formulae for calculating great circle courses and distances are derived from the same formulae which are used to find calculated altitudes and azimuths. The formulae for great circle distance are:

$$\cos d = \sin \text{Lat}_1 \sin \text{Lat}_2 + \cos \text{Lat}_1 \cos \text{Lat}_2 \cos d.\text{Long}$$
$$\text{distance} = 60d$$

where $\text{Lat}_1$ and $\text{Lat}_2$ are the latitudes of the starting and finishing points, and d.Long is the difference in longitude between the two points.

The great circle course changes throughout the passage as it curves across the Mercator chart meridians at different angles. In practice the initial course angle is calculated and a rhumb line course is then sailed at that angle for a certain distance. From that point a new great circle initial course is calculated and a new rhumb line course is sailed at the new angle. This procedure is repeated throughout the passage so that a great circle track is followed as a series of different rhumb line courses. The formula for the initial great circle course is:

Course = polar co-ordinate angle of rectangular co-ordinates x and y

where $x = \cos \text{Lat}_1 \tan \text{Lat}_2 - \sin \text{Lat}_1 \cos d.\text{Long}$
$y = \sin d.\text{Long}$

*Example*
What is the great circle distance from Bergen to Aberdeen?

$$\text{Distance} = 60d$$
$$\cos d = \sin \text{Lat}_1 \sin \text{Lat}_2 + \cos \text{Lat}_1 \cos \text{Lat}_2 \cos d.\text{Long}$$

$\text{Lat}_1 = 60° \, 23'\text{N}$ $\text{Lat}_2 = 57° \, 08'\text{N}$ $d.\text{Long} = 2° \, 04'\text{W} - 5° \, 27'\text{E}$
$$= -2° \, 04' - 5° \, 27'$$
$$= -7° \, 31'$$

$\cos d = \sin 60.3833 \times \sin 57.1333 + \cos 60.3833 \times$
$\cos 57.1333 \times \cos -7.5167$
$= 0.9961$
$d = 5°.0703$
$\text{Distance} = 5.0703 \times 60$
$= 304.2180'$
$= 304 \, miles$

Comparing this result with the previous example it can be seen that the great circle and rhumb line distances are virtually identical over a distance of 300 miles. The great circle course is less than half a mile shorter than the rhumb line.

*Example*
What is the great circle distance and initial course from Port Stanley to Cape Town? Compare this with the rhumb line course and distance.

Port Stanley: 51° 40'S 58°W      Cape Town: 33° 55'S 18° 22'E

*Great Circle Passage*

$$\text{d.Long} = 18.3667 - (-58)$$
$$= 76°.3667$$

$$\cos d = \sin -51.6667 \times \sin -33.9167 + \cos -51.6667 \times \cos -33.9167 \times \cos 76.3667$$
$$= 0.5590$$
$$d = 56°.0125$$
$$60d = 3360.7475'$$

*Great Circle Distance = 3361 miles*

$$\text{Course} = \text{polar co-ordinate angle of R} \to \text{P} \quad x \text{ and } y$$
$$x = \cos \text{Lat}_1 \tan \text{Lat}_2 - \sin \text{Lat}_1 \cos \text{d.Long}$$
$$= \cos -51.6667 \times \tan -33.9167 - \sin -51.6667 \times \cos 76.3667$$
$$= -0.2322$$
$$y = \sin \text{d.Long}$$
$$= \sin 76.3667$$
$$= 0.9718$$

$$\text{Polar co-ordinate angle} = \text{R} \to \text{P} \quad -0.2322 \quad 0.9718$$
$$= 103°.4351$$

*Initial Course = 103°*

*Rhumb Line Passage*

$$\text{d.Long} = 60 \times 76°.3667$$
$$= 4582.0020'$$
$$\text{d.Lat} = 60 \times (-33°.9167 - (-51°.6667))$$
$$= 1065'$$

$$\text{M Pts destination} = 7915.7 \log \tan(45 + 0.5 \times (-33.9167)) - 23.27 \times \sin -33.9167$$
$$= -2152.4669$$

| M Pts start | $=$ | $7915.7 \log \tan(45 + 0.5 \times (-51.6667) - 23.27 \times \sin -51.6667$ |
| | $=$ | $-3614.5734$ |
| DMP | $=$ | $-2152.4669 - (-3614.5734)$ |
| | $=$ | $1462.1065$ |
| Course | $=$ | R→P   DMP       d.Long |
| | $=$ | R→P   1462.1065   4582.0020 |
| | $=$ | $72°.3022$ |
| Distance | $=$ | d.Lat/cos course |
| | $=$ | $1065 \div \cos 72.3022$ |
| | $=$ | $3503.3300$ |

*Rhumb Line Passage*   $=$   *072° 3503 miles*

This example shows that the difference between rhumb line and great circle distances is quite large over such a long passage. It amounts to 142 miles, equivalent to a day's sailing. Thus it is obvious that for long distances a great circle course is significantly shorter.

In all these calculations, rhumb line and great circle, it is necessary to find the difference in longitude. The formula is:

d.Long   $=$   destination Long $-$ start Long

However, there is one exception to this rule: where the passage crosses the meridian 180°, eg from 170°W to 170°E. In this case the difference in longitude is obviously 20°, but if the original formula were used it would be:

| d.Long | $=$ | $170 - (-170)$ |
| | $=$ | $340°$ |

It is therefore necessary to use a different formula when crossing the 180° meridian. In such cases, west longitude must be expressed as *east* longitude by subtracting from 360. Thus:

| 170°W | $=$ | $360 - 170$ |
| | $=$ | $190°E$ |

Using the same example of a passage from 170°W to 170°E, the formula becomes:

| d.Long | $=$ | destination Long $-$ start Long |
| | $=$ | $170°E - 170°W$ |
| | $=$ | $170 - (360 - 170)$ |
| | $=$ | $-20°$ |

*Example*
What is the rhumb line course and distance from Sydney to Honolulu?

Sydney: 33° 53'S 151° 10'E      Honolulu: 21° 19'N 157° 52'W

| d.Long | = | Long Honolulu − Long Sydney |
|---|---|---|
| | = | 157°.8667W − 151°.1667E |
| | = | (360 − 157.8667) − 151.1667 |
| | = | 50°.9666 |
| | = | 3057.9960' |

| d.Lat | = | 21°.3167 − (−33°.8833) |
|---|---|---|
| | = | 55°.2000 |
| | = | 3312' |

| M Pts Sydney | = | 7915.7 log tan(45 + 0.5 × (−33.8833) − 23.27 × sin −33.8833 |
|---|---|---|
| | = | −2150.0686 |

| M Pts Honolulu | = | 7915.7 log tan(45 + 0.5 × 21.3167) − 23.27 × sin 21.3167 |
|---|---|---|
| | = | 1301.1102 |

| DMP | = | 3451.1788 |
|---|---|---|

| Course | = | R→P   DMP      d.Long' |
|---|---|---|
| | = | R→P   3451.1788     3057.9960 |
| | = | *41°.5433* |

| Distance | = | d.Lat'/cos course |
|---|---|---|
| | = | 3312 ÷ cos 41.5433 |
| | = | *4425.1172* |

*Rhumb Line*  =  *042° 4425 miles*

## Summary

*Difference in Longitude*

d.Long  =  destination Long − start Long

where passage crosses 180° meridian:

Longitude West  =  360 − Long

*Rhumb Line*

Under 500 miles = R→P  d.Lat'   departure
       d.Lat  =  destination Lat − start Lat
   departure =  d.Long cos mean Lat

Over 500 miles

| | | |
|---|---|---|
| Course | = | polar co-ordinate angle of R→P x and y |
| x | = | DMP |
| y | = | d.Long (minutes) |
| DMP | = | M Pts destination − M Pts start |
| M Pts | = | $7915.7 \log \tan(45 + 0.5 \text{Lat}) - 23.27 \sin \text{Lat}$ |
| Distance | = | d.Lat'/cos course |

*Great Circle*

| | | |
|---|---|---|
| Distance | = | 60d |
| cos d | = | $\sin \text{Lat}_1 \sin \text{Lat}_2 + \cos \text{Lat}_1 \cos \text{Lat}_2$ cos d.Long |
| Initial course | = | polar co-ordinate angle of R→P x and y |
| x | = | $\cos \text{Lat}_1 \tan \text{Lat}_2 - \sin \text{Lat}_1 \cos \text{d.Long}$ |
| y | = | sin d.Long |
| where $\text{Lat}_1$ | = | latitude of starting point |
| $\text{Lat}_2$ | = | latitude of finishing point |

**Exercise 10** (Answers in Appendix C)

1 What is the rhumb line course and distance from Felixstowe 51° 57′N 1° 18′E to Zeebrugge 51° 20′N 3° 12′E? (Under 500 miles)
2 What is the rhumb line course and distance from Mombassa 4° 02′S 39° 43′E to Bombay 18° 55′N 72° 50′E? (Over 500 miles)
3 What is the great circle distance and initial course from Colombo 6° 56′N 79° 58′E to Fremantle 31° 01′S 115° 47′E?
4 What is the great circle distance and initial course from Honolulu 21° 19′N 157° 52′W to Tokyo 35° 45′N 139° 45′E?
5 Compare the great circle and rhumb line routes from Ascension 8°S 14° 15′W to Port Stanley 51° 40′S 58°W.

# 13

# Identification of Stars and Planets

Sextant sights of heavenly bodies are followed by calculation of their geographical position, as shown in Chapter 4. Sun and moon sights present no problem but there may well be some uncertainty about the identity of an observed star or planet, and without positive identification a valid position line is unobtainable. The practical problem facing a navigator is the limited time available for star sights. They must be confined to twilight as this is the only time when stars and the horizon are visible together. Beyond twilight it is either too light or too dark to see both together.

With clear skies there is no difficulty identifying stars as entire constellations are visible and star charts can be used if necessary. But if the sky is obscured by clouds there may only be fleeting glimpses of isolated stars. It can be extremely difficult to identify stars under such conditions, and the same applies to planets. However, it does not matter if immediate identification is impossible. As long as the star is bright enough to be on the list of navigational stars, all that is required is the sextant altitude and exact time of the sight and a compass bearing of the star or planet.

## Stars

The list of navigational stars in RGO tables and nautical almanacs gives their sidereal hour angle (SHA) and declination; so that if these values could be calculated, they would identify an unknown star. The required information for calculating SHA and declination is the estimated position (EP) of the yacht at the time of sight, sextant altitude of the star and its compass bearing. The formula for calculating declination is:

$$\sin Dec = \sin Lat \sin Ho + \cos Lat \cos Ho \cos Az$$

where Dec is declination; Az is the true compass bearing; Lat is the EP latitude; and Ho is the true sextant altitude.

Having found declination, the next steps are to find the local hour angles of Aries (LHAγ) and the unknown star (LHA*).

$$LHA\gamma = GHA\gamma + EP \, Long$$

GHAγ is found from RGO tables as shown in Chapter 4.
LHA* is found from the following formula:

77

$$\cos \text{LHA*} \quad = \quad (\sin \text{Ho} - \sin \text{Lat} \sin \text{Dec})/(\cos \text{Lat} \cos \text{Dec})$$

Having found LHAγ and LHA*
if sin Az is less than zero
SHA   =   LHA* − LHAγ
but if sin Az is greater than zero
SHA   =   360 − LHA* − LHAγ

*Example*

At 1830 GMT on 22 September 1981 at EP 52° 10′N 02° 15′E, a sextant sight of an unknown star gave a true altitude of 28° 58′. Its compass bearing was 265°T. Identify the star.

For the purpose of identification it is only necessary to find the approximate declination and SHA. All the variables can be rounded to the nearest degree as follows:

Az = 265°      Ho = 29°      EP Lat = 52°      EP Long = 2°

| | | |
|---|---|---|
| Sin Dec | = | sin Lat sin Ho + cos Lat cos Ho cos Az |
| | = | sin 52 × sin 29 + cos 52 × cos 29 × cos 265 |
| | = | 0.3351 |
| *Dec* | = | *19.5789* (memory 1) |
| LHAγ | = | GHAγ + EP Long |
| GHAγ | = | A + 0.985647x + 15 GMT |
| x | = | date + GMT/24 |
| | = | 22 + 18.5 ÷ 24 |
| | = | 22.7708 |

From RGO tables (see Appendix B)

| | | |
|---|---|---|
| A | = | 339.0871 |
| LHAγ | = | 339.0871 + 0.985647 × 22.7708 + 15 × 18.5 + 2 |
| | = | 641.0311 (−360) |
| | = | 281.0311 (memory 2) |
| cos LHA* | = | (sin Ho − sin Lat sin Dec)/(cos Lat cos Dec) |
| | = | (sin 29 − sin 52 × sin memory 1) ÷ (cos 52 × cos memory 1) |
| | = | 0.3806 |
| LHA* | = | 67.6322 (memory 3) |
| sin Az | = | sin 265 |
| | = | −0.9962 |

As sin Az is less than zero

| | | |
|---|---|---|
| SHA | = | LHA* − LHAγ |
| | = | memory 3 − memory 2 |
| | = | −213.3989 (+360) |
| | = | *146.6011* |

Thus the approximate SHA and declination of the unknown star are 146.6 and 19°.6N. Now turn to RGO tables (Appendix B) where the navigational stars are listed in order of approximate SHA. The only star with an SHA of 146° is Arcturus. Next check the approximate declination of Arcturus. This again corresponds with our calculated declination of 19°.6N and confirms that the observed star was indeed Arcturus.

Having confirmed the star's identity, the true azimuth and intercept are then calculated as shown in Chapters 4 and 5.

**Planets**
There are only four navigational planets: Venus, Jupiter, Mars and Saturn; but they can pose more of a problem than stars as they do not have a fixed position relative to the constellations. On the other hand they can often be observed in daylight, as they are much brighter than stars, so the time available for sights is greater. If an unknown planet is sighted, its identity can be confirmed by taking its sextant altitude and recording the exact time. As in the case of unknown stars, a compass bearing is also required. The GHA and declination of the four navigational planets is then found from RGO tables, after which the azimuth and altitude of each is calculated. The results are compared with the observed altitude and compass bearing; and the unknown planet can then be identified as the one whose observed and calculated values correspond.

*Example*
At 1700 GMT on 15 December 1981, at EP 52°N 02°E, a sextant sight of an unknown planet gave a true altitude of 11° 30′. Its compass bearing was 210°T. Identify the planet.

1 From RGO tables (Appendix B) calculate the GHA and declination of each planet at 1700 GMT.
2 Calculate the altitude (Hc) and azimuth (Az) of each planet.
3 Compare these with the observed altitude and compass bearing to identify the planet.

|      | *Venus* | *Jupiter* | *Mars* | *Saturn* |
|------|---------|-----------|--------|----------|
| Lat  | 52      | 52        | 52     | 52       |
| Long | 2       | 2         | 2      | 2        |
| GMT  | 17      | 17        | 17     | 17       |
| x    | 0.4909  | 0.4909    | 0.4909 | 0.4909   |
| GHA  | 32.3402 | 127.6323  | 158.5490 | 139.5273 |
| LHA  | 34.3402 | 129.6323  | 160.5490 | 141.5273 |
| Dec  | −20.6748 | −11.5984 | 1.9961 | −5.7821  |
| Hc   | 11.3848 | −32.8960  | −33.5541 | −33.9826 |
| Az   | 212.5728 |          |        |          |

The only planet corresponding with the observed altitude and bearing is Venus. Having identified the planet and already calculated its altitude and azimuth, the intercept can be found and a position line obtained. In this example the other three planets gave a negative altitude. This means that they were all below the horizon at that time so there is no point in calculating their azimuths.

## Summary

*Unknown star*
1 Take sextant sight and compass bearing. Record time.
2 sin Dec = sin Lat sin Ho + cos Lat cos Ho cos Az
3 cos LHA* = (sin Ho − sin Lat sin Dec)/(cos Lat cos Dec)
4 Calculate LHAγ
5 If sin Az<0     SHA = LHA* − LHAγ
  If sin Az>0     SHA = 360 − LHA* − LHAγ
6 Compare SHA and Dec with list of navigational stars.

*Unknown planet*
1 Take sextant sight and compass bearing. Record time.
2 Calculate GHA and Dec of Venus, Jupiter, Mars and Saturn.
3 Calculate Hc and Az for each.
4 Compare Hc and Az with Ho and compass bearing.

**Exercise 11** (Answers in Appendix C)

1 At 1700 GMT on 6 September 1981, at EP 35°N 35°E, the altitude of an unknown star was 62° bearing 060°T. Identify the star.
2 At 0530 GMT on 30 September 1981, at EP 51° 18′N 1° 40′E, the altitude of an unknown planet bearing 115°T was 39°. Identify the planet.
3 At EP 28°N 88°W on 24 July 1981, two unidentified stars were observed: at 1900 LT bearing 092°T, altitude 22° 10′; at 1903 LT bearing 160°T, altitude 33° 12′. Fix the yacht's position.
4 On 27 December 1981 at EP 53° 42′N 4° 50′W an unknown star was observed at 08h06m05s GMT bearing 255°T, altitude 26° 37′. At 08h08m26s GMT the meridian altitude of an unknown planet, bearing south, was 24° 15′. Fix the yacht's position.
5 On 15 October 1981 at 04h32m27s GMT, at EP 34° 08′N 14° 22′E, the altitude of an unknown star bearing 190°T was 39° 08′. The yacht then made good a course and distance of 275°, 4 miles when at 05h02m48s GMT the altitude of the moon was 23° 12′. Fix the yacht's position.

# 14

# Sextant Sights

All the previous calculations have used the symbol Ho which means the true observed altitude of a heavenly body. This is not the same thing as the sextant altitude taken by the observer. It is the altitude obtained after various corrections have been applied to the sextant altitude taken by the observer.

It is not proposed to complicate this book by discussing the theory of sextant sights and all their corrections; or how to adjust a sextant. This has already been well covered in other books and there is no need here to delve too deeply into the reasons for these corrections. Sextant adjustment is also covered in the instruction booklets provided by manufacturers.

## Corrections

When the yachtsman has taken a sextant sight, various corrections must be applied before it represents the **true altitude** of the observed heavenly body. The first correction to be applied is for optical error of the instrument itself. This is called **index error**. The next correction allows for the height of the observer's eye above his horizon. This is called **dip**. After correcting the original sextant altitude for index error and dip, the resultant figure is called the **apparent altitude**. This in turn has to be corrected for **refraction** of light passing through the atmosphere and for horizontal parallax. In the case of the sun and moon the observation must also be corrected for their semi-diameter, and whether the sextant has measured to their upper or lower edge, or limb as it is called. All these corrections to the original sextant altitude will be handled by calculator to produce the True Altitude Ho.

## Index Error

This is checked each time the sextant is used. If there were no index error, the reflected and direct images of the observed body would coincide exactly when the sextant angle reads zero. Usually, however, some discrepancy is apparent and is corrected by turning the micrometer drum. When the images coincide the micrometer reading gives the index error. A sextant scale reads down from 120° through 0° to −10°. If the scale reading is negative, ie less than 0°, the index error is read from the micrometer drum as a negative quantity, eg −5′. If the sextant scale reading is more than 0°, the error is read from the micrometer drum as a positive quantity, eg 5′.

The calculator formula for correcting sextant altitude for index error is:

$$\text{sextant altitude} - \text{index error}$$

eg sextant altitude 30° 30′     index error 5′

$$= \quad 30° 30′ - 5′$$
$$= \quad 30° 25′$$

If the index error is −5′

$$\text{altitude} \quad = \quad 30° 30′ - (-5′)$$
$$= \quad 30° 35′$$

## Dip

Dip is a correction applied to the sextant altitude to allow for the height of the observer's eye above the horizon. It is subtracted from the sextant altitude and is found from the formula:

$$D \quad = \quad 0.0293 \sqrt{h}$$

where D  =  dip (in degrees)
      h  =  height of eye (in metres)

eg height of eye 2.5m
$$D \quad = \quad 0.0293 \sqrt{2.5}$$
$$= \quad 0.0463$$

## Apparent Altitude

Apparent altitude is the sextant altitude corrected for index error and dip. The formula for obtaining the apparent altitude is:

$$H \quad = \quad Hs - IE - D$$

where H  =  apparent altitude
     Hs  =  sextant altitude
     IE  =  index error
     D  =  dip

but D  =  $0.0293 \sqrt{h}$, so the formula now becomes:

$$H \quad = \quad Hs - IE - 0.0293 \sqrt{h}$$

where h  =  height of eye in metres.

*Example*
Find the apparent altitude of sextant sight 30° 30′, IE −5′, height of eye 2.5m.

$$H = Hs - IE - 0.0293 \sqrt{h}$$

| | | |
|---|---|---|
| Hs (decimalised) | = | 30°.5 |
| IE (degrees) | = | −0°.0833 |

$$H = 30.5 - (-0.0833) - 0.0293 \times 1.5811$$
$$= 30°.5370$$

Thus the apparent altitude is 30°.5370.

Having obtained the apparent altitude, the true altitude is found by further calculations as follows. However, it may also be found by using the correction tables in nautical almanacs; and yachtsmen may well prefer to do that instead of using a calculator.

## Refraction

Refraction is a correction which allows for the bending of light rays as they enter the earth's atmosphere from heavenly bodies in outer space. Refraction is subtracted from the apparent altitude.

For altitudes greater than 15° the formula is:

$$R = 0.0162 \tan(90 - H)$$

where R is refraction and H is apparent altitude.

For altitudes less than 15° the formula is:

$$R = (0.5743 + 0.0705H + 0.00007H^2)/(1 + 0.505H + 0.0845H^2)$$

*Examples*
1 Find the refraction for an apparent altitude of 40°

$$R = 0.0162 \tan(90 - H)$$
$$= 0.0162 \times \tan 50$$
$$= 0.0193$$

2 Find the refraction for an apparent altitude of 11°

$$R = (0.5743 + 0.0705H + 0.00007H^2)/(1 + 0.505H + 0.0845H^2)$$
$$= (0.5743 + 0.0705 \times 11 + 0.00007 \times 121) \div (1 + 0.505 \times 11 + 0.0845 \times 121)$$
$$= 1.3583 \div 16.7795$$
$$= 0.0809$$

In practice, altitudes below 10° are considered unreliable as

refraction error is greatest with low altitudes. Extremes of tempera-
ture and pressure also affect refraction and the RGO tables do
include a formula for making this correction. However, as far as
yachtsmen are concerned, this extra correction is rarely needed and
is of little practical consequence unless very low altitudes are
involved.

## Stars, Jupiter and Saturn

Sextant sights of stars, and the planets Jupiter and Saturn, only need
correction for refraction. Thus the formula for the true observed
altitude of a star is:

$$Ho = H - R$$

where Ho is the true observed altitude, H apparent altitude and R
refraction.

In a previous example the apparent altitude was 30°.5370. In
practice this would be stored in the calculator's memory, so in this
case the calculation would be:

$$
\begin{aligned}
R &= 0.0162 \times \tan(90 - 30.5370) \\
&= 0.0275 \\
Ho &= 30.5370 - 0.0275 \\
&= 30°.5095
\end{aligned}
$$

*Example*
1 Sextant altitude star Procyon 25° 29′, IE 1′, height of eye 2m.
Find the true observed altitude.

$$
\begin{aligned}
H &= Hs - IE - 0.0293 \sqrt{h} \\
&= 25.4833 - 0.0167 - 0.0293 \times 1.4142 \\
&= 25°.4252
\end{aligned}
$$

This is the apparent altitude and is stored in memory 1. Now
continue:

$$
\begin{aligned}
R &= 0.0162 \tan(90 - H) \\
&= 0.0162 \times \tan(90 - \text{memory 1}) \\
&= 0.0341 \,(\text{memory 2}) \\
Ho &= H - R \\
&= \text{memory 1} - \text{memory 2} \\
&= 25°.3912
\end{aligned}
$$

*True observed altitude is 25°.3912*

2 Sextant altitude Jupiter 42° 37.7′, IE 4′, height of eye 2.4m.
Find the true observed altitude.

84

$$
\begin{aligned}
H &= 42.6283 - 0.0667 - 0.0293 \times 1.5492 \\
&= 42°.5163 \,(\text{memory } 1)
\end{aligned}
$$

$$
\begin{aligned}
R &= 0.0162 \times \tan(90 - \text{memory } 1) \\
&= 0.0177 \,(\text{memory } 2)
\end{aligned}
$$

$$
\begin{aligned}
Ho &= \text{memory } 1 - \text{memory } 2 \\
&= 42°.4986
\end{aligned}
$$

### Mars and Venus

An extra correction for horizontal parallax (HP) must be applied to the sun and moon and the planets Mars and Venus. It is not applied to the stars or other planets as they are sufficiently far away. The formula for Mars and Venus is:

$$Ho = H + HP \cos H - R$$

where Ho = true observed altitude
H = apparent altitude
HP = horizontal parallax
R = refraction

Values for horizontal parallax are given in RGO tables.

*Example*
28 December 1981, sextant altitude Venus 21° 11′, IE −6′, height of eye 3m. Find the true observed altitude.
From RGO tables (Appendix B), HP Venus = 0.007

$$
\begin{aligned}
Ho &= H + HP \cos H - R
\end{aligned}
$$

$$
\begin{aligned}
H &= 21.1833 - (-0.1) - 0.0293 \times 1.7231 \\
&= 21°.2326 \,(\text{memory } 1)
\end{aligned}
$$

$$
\begin{aligned}
HP \cos H &= 0.007 \times \cos \text{memory } 1 \\
&= 0.0065 \,(\text{memory } 2)
\end{aligned}
$$

$$
\begin{aligned}
R &= 0.0162 \times \tan(90 - \text{memory } 1) \\
&= 0.0417 \,(\text{memory } 3)
\end{aligned}
$$

$$
\begin{aligned}
Ho &= \text{memory } 1 + \text{memory } 2 - \text{memory } 3 \\
&= 21°.1974
\end{aligned}
$$

### Sun

The sun's horizontal parallax is a constant 0.0024 but another correction must be applied for its semi-diameter (S). This value is given in the RGO tables. Semi-diameter correction allows for the fact that a sextant measures to the edge and not the centre of a disc.

The formula is:

$$Ho = H \pm S + HP \cos H - R$$
$$= H \pm S + 0.0024 \cos H - R$$

Semi-diameter S is added if the lower limb (LL) is observed but subtracted for the upper limb (UL). Thus for a lower limb observation the formula is:

$$Ho = H + S + 0.0024 \cos H - R$$

*Example*
10 December 1981, sextant altitude sun LL 18° 30′, IE 2′, height of eye 3.5m. Find the true observed altitude.
From RGO tables (Appendix B) S = 0.271

$$H = 18.5 - 0.0333 - 0.0293 \times 1.8708$$
$$= 18°.4119$$

$$R = 0.0162 \times \tan 71.5881$$
$$= 0.0487$$

$$Ho = 18.4119 + 0.271 + 0.0024 \times \cos 18.4119 - 0.0487$$
$$= \textit{18°.6365}$$

## Moon

As in the case of the sun, both horizontal parallax and semi-diameter corrections are applied to the apparent altitude of the moon. The formula is:

$$Ho = H \pm S + (HP - 0.0017) \cos H - R$$

where semi-diameter S = 0.2724 HP and, like the sun, is added for lower limb observations but subtracted for the upper limb. Horizontal parallax varies hourly and must be separately calculated from the tables. The formula is:

$$HP = a_1 x + a_0$$

where $x = GMT/24$
and values $a_1$ and $a_0$ are given in the RGO tables.

*Example*
12 December 1981 at 0800 GMT, sextant altitude Moon UL 9° 10′, IE 5′, height of eye 4m. Find the true observed altitude.

$$Ho = H - 0.2724\,HP + (HP - 0.0017) \cos H - R$$

$$H = 9.1667 - 0.0833 - 0.0293 \times 2$$
$$= 9°.0247$$

RGO tables (Appendix B)      $a_0 = 1.0218$      $a_1 = -0.0083$

HP      $=\;\; -0.0083 \times 8 \div 24 + 1.0218$

      $=\;\;\;\; 1.0190$

R (<15)  $=\;\;$ $(0.5743 + 0.0705 \times 9.0247 + 0.00007 \times$
      $81.4452) \div (1 + 0.505 \times 9.0247 + 0.0845 \times$
      $81.4452)$

      $=\;\;$ $0.0978$

Ho      $=\;\;$ $9.0247 - 0.2724 \times 1.0190 + (1.0190 - 0.0017) \times$
      $\cos 9.0247 - 0.0978$

      $=\;\;$ *9.6541*

## Summary

Hs   $=$   original sextant altitude
H   $=$   apparent altitude
Ho   $=$   true observed altitude
IE   $=$   index error (degrees)
D   $=$   dip
h   $=$   height of eye (metres)
HP   $=$   horizontal parallax
S   $=$   semi-diameter
UL   $=$   upper limb $(-)$
LL   $=$   lower limb $(+)$
R   $=$   refraction

D   $=$   $0.0293 \sqrt{h}$
H   $=$   $Hs - IE - D$
   $=$   $Hs - IE - 0.0293 \sqrt{h}$

H >15°  R  $=$   $0.0162 \tan(90 - H)$
H <15°  R  $=$   $(0.5743 + 0.0705H + 0.00007H^2)/(1 + 0.505H + 0.0845H^2)$

*Stars, Jupiter, Saturn*

   Ho   $=$   $H - R$

*Mars, Venus*

   Ho   $=$   $H + HP \cos H - R$

*Sun*

LL  Ho  $=$   $H + S + 0.0024 \cos H - R$
UL  Ho  $=$   $H - S + 0.0024 \cos H - R$

*Moon*

$$HP = a_1 x + a_0 \qquad x = GMT/24$$
$$LL \quad Ho = H + 0.2724\,HP + (HP - 0.0017)\cos H - R$$
$$UL \quad Ho = H - 0.2724\,HP + (HP - 0.0017)\cos H - R$$

**Exercise 12** (Answers in Appendix C)

1 The sextant altitude of a heavenly body was 23° 59', IE −4', height of eye 4.5m. What is the apparent altitude?
2 The sextant altitude of star Aldebaran was 37° 46', IE 2', height of eye 2.8m. Find the true altitude.
3 The sextant altitude of Mars on 27 December 1981 was 30° 14', IE −4', height of eye 6m. Find the true altitude.
4 On 10 October 1981 at 05h45m16s GMT, the sextant altitude of the moon, upper limb, was 58° 37', IE 0, height of eye 3m. What was the true observed altitude?
5 On 2 September 1981, the sextant altitude of the sun, lower limb, was 42° 02', IE −3', height of eye 3.6m. Find the true altitude.

# Appendix A
# Summary of Formulae

**Estimated Position**

$$EP = \begin{array}{l} \text{fix Lat} + \text{d.Lat} \\ \text{fix Long} + \text{d.long} \end{array}$$

$$\begin{array}{l} \text{d.Lat} \\ \text{departure} \end{array} = \text{P} \rightarrow \text{R course and distance made good}$$

Course and distance made good = total of rectangular co-ordinates:
courses steered
distances logged
tidal sets
tidal drifts

$$\text{d.Long} = \text{departure/cos(d.Lat/2 + fix Lat)}$$

**Geographical Position**

*Sun and Planets*

$$
\begin{aligned}
\text{GHA} &= 15((((a_4x + a_3)x + a_2)x + a_1)x + a_0 + \text{GMT}) \\
\text{Dec} &= (((a_4x + a_3)x + a_2)x + a_1)x + a_0 \\
x &= (\text{date} + \text{GMT}/24)/32
\end{aligned}
$$

*Moon*

$$
\begin{aligned}
\text{GHA, Dec} &= (a_2 + a_1)x + a_0 \\
x &= \text{GMT}/24
\end{aligned}
$$

*Stars*

$$
\begin{aligned}
\text{GHA}^* &= \text{GHA}\gamma + \text{SHA} \\
\text{GHA}\gamma &= A + 0.985647x + 15\text{GMT} \\
\text{SHA, Dec} &= a_0 + 0.0001(a_1 + a_2x) \\
x &= \text{date} + \text{GMT}/24
\end{aligned}
$$

### Altitude, Azimuth and Intercept

$$\text{LHA} = \text{GHA} + \text{Long}$$

*Altitude*

$$\sin \text{Hc} = \sin \text{Lat} \sin \text{Dec} + \cos \text{Lat} \cos \text{Dec} \cos \text{LHA}$$

*Azimuth*

$$\text{Az} = \text{polar co-ordinate angle of x and y}$$
$$x = \cos \text{Lat} \sin \text{Dec} - \sin \text{Lat} \cos \text{Dec} \cos \text{LHA}$$
$$y = -\cos \text{Dec} \sin \text{LHA}$$

*Intercept*

$$p = \text{Ho} - \text{Hc}$$

### Fix

$$\text{Fix} = \begin{matrix} \text{EP Lat} + \text{d.Lat} \\ \text{EP Long} + \text{d.Long} \end{matrix}$$

$$\text{d.Lat} = (DC - EB)/G$$
$$\text{d.Long} = (AE - BD)/(G \cos \text{EP Lat})$$

| | | | |
|---|---|---|---|
| A | = total of | $\cos^2 \text{Az}$ | for each sight |
| B | = total of | $\cos \text{Az} \sin \text{Az}$ | for each sight |
| C | = total of | $\sin^2 \text{Az}$ | for each sight |
| D | = total of | $p \cos \text{Az}$ | for each sight |
| E | = total of | $p \sin \text{Az}$ | for each sight |

$$\text{Check } A + C = \text{number of sights}$$
$$G = AC - B^2$$

### Running Fix

$$\text{Fix} = \begin{matrix} \text{EP}_2 \text{ Lat} + \text{d.Lat} \\ \text{EP}_2 \text{ Long} + \text{d.Long} \end{matrix}$$

### Latitude by Meridian Altitude

$$\text{True latitude} = 90 + \text{Ho} + \text{Dec} (-180)$$

$$\text{where Ho} = \text{meridian altitude bearing} \begin{cases} \text{north positive} \\ \text{south negative} \end{cases}$$

$$p = \text{true latitude} - \text{EP latitude}$$
$$\text{Az} = 360°$$

## Latitude by Polaris

| | | |
|---|---|---|
| SHA Polaris | $=$ | $70(a_0 + 0.0001(a_1 + a_2x))$ |
| Polar Distance (p) | $=$ | $a_0 + 0.0001(a_1 + a_2x)$ |
| x | $=$ | date + GMT/24 |
| LHA Polaris | $=$ | GHA$\gamma$ + SHA + EP Long |
| C | $=$ | p cos LHA |
| S | $=$ | p sin LHA |
| True Latitude | $=$ | $Ho - C + 0.0087\, S^2 \tan Ho$ |
| Azimuth | $=$ | $-S/\cos Ho$ (Use 360° in practice) |
| Intercept p | $=$ | True Lat $-$ EP Lat |

## Identification of Stars

$$\sin Dec = \sin Lat \sin Ho + \cos Lat \cos Ho \cos Az$$
$$\cos LHA^* = (\sin Ho - \sin Lat \sin Dec)/(\cos Lat \cos Dec)$$

if sin Az is less than zero     SHA $=$ LHA$^*$ $-$ LHA$\gamma$
if sin Az is more than zero     SHA $=$ 360 $-$ LHA$^*$ $-$ LHA$\gamma$

## Time

| | | |
|---|---|---|
| LT | $=$ | GMT + Long$^h$ |
| GMT | $=$ | LT $-$ Long$^h$ |
| Long$^h$ | $=$ | Long/15 |
| ZT | $=$ | GMT $-$ Zone |
| GMT | $=$ | ZT + Zone |

## Course and Distance
*Difference in Longitude*

$$d.Long = \text{destination Long} - \text{start Long}$$

but where passage crosses 180° meridian:

$$\text{Longitude West} = 360 - Long$$

*Rhumb Line*

| | | |
|---|---|---|
| Under 500 miles | $=$ | R$\rightarrow$P  d.Lat$'$  dep |
| d.Lat | $=$ | destination Lat $-$ start Lat |
| dep | $=$ | d.long cos mean Lat |

Over 500 miles

| | | |
|---|---|---|
| Course | = | polar co-ordinate angle of R→P x and y |
| x | = | DMP |
| y | = | d.Long' |
| DMP | = | M Pts destination − M Pts start |
| M Pts | = | $7915.7 \log \tan(45 + 0.5 \text{ Lat}) - 23.27 \sin \text{Lat}$ |
| Distance | = | d.Lat'/cos course |

*Great Circle*

| | | |
|---|---|---|
| $\text{Lat}_1$ | = | latitude of starting point |
| $\text{Lat}_2$ | = | latitude of finishing point |
| Distance | = | 60d |
| cos d | = | $\sin \text{Lat}_1 \sin \text{Lat}_2 + \cos \text{Lat}_1 \cos \text{Lat}_2 \cos \text{d.Long}$ |
| Initial course | = | polar co-ordinate angle of R→P x and y |
| x | = | $\cos \text{Lat}_1 \tan \text{Lat}_2 - \sin \text{Lat}_1 \cos \text{d.Long}$ |
| y | = | sin d.Long |

## Sextant Altitude Corrections (Hs to Ho)

*Apparent Altitude* (H)

$$H = Hs - IE - 0.0293 \sqrt{h}$$

*Refraction* (R)

H >15   $R = 0.0162 \tan(90 - H)$

H <15   $R = (0.5743 + 0.0705 H + 0.00007 H^2)/(1 + 0.505 H + 0.0845 H^2)$

*Stars, Jupiter and Saturn*

$$Ho = H - R$$

*Mars and Venus*

$$Ho = H + HP \cos H - R$$

*Sun*

$$LL \quad Ho = H + S + 0.0024 \cos H - R$$
$$UL \quad Ho = H - S + 0.0024 \cos H - R$$

*Moon*

$$HP = a_1 x + a_0$$
$$x = GMT/24$$

LL   Ho = $H + 0.2724 HP + (HP - 0.0017) \cos H - R$
UL   Ho = $H - 0.2724 HP + (HP - 0.0017) \cos H - R$

# Appendix B
# Tables

The following tables are extracts from the Royal Greenwich Observatory Bulletin No. 185, 'Compact Data for Navigation and Astronomy for 1981 to 1985'. They are reproduced with permission, from data supplied by the Science and Engineering Research Council.

Table 4: GHA ARIES

Monthly Coefficient A

|        | 1981     |
|--------|----------|
|        | o        |
| Jan.   | 99.5748  |
| Feb.   | 130.1299 |
| Mar.   | 157.7280 |
| Apr.   | 188.2831 |
| May    | 217.8525 |
| June   | 248.4076 |
| July   | 277.9770 |
| Aug.   | 308.5321 |
| Sep.   | 339.0871 |
| Oct.   | 8.65.6   |
| Nov.   | 39.2116  |
| Dec.   | 68.7810  |

GHA Aries = $A + 0.985647x + 15GMT^h$ where $x = d + GMT^h/24$ and $d$ = day of month

## Table 2: MOON, 1981

| Day | | October | | | November | | | December | |
|---|---|---|---|---|---|---|---|---|---|
| | | GHA° | DEC° | HP° | GHA° | DEC° | HP° | GHA° | DEC° | HP° |
| 1 | a0 | 150.8184 | -10.0017 | 0.9061 | 136.9023 | -20.6343 | 0.9011 | 131.2855 | -19.1637 | 0.9120 |
| | a1 | 349.4927 | -3.9255 | -0.0034 | 348.4383 | -1.4367 | 0.0039 | 348.0643 | 1.2221 | 0.0079 |
| | a2 | -0.1005 | 0.2524 | | -0.1237 | 0.4683 | | 0.0444 | 0.4851 | |
| 2 | a0 | 140.2097 | -13.6735 | 0.9027 | 125.2178 | -21.6021 | 0.9050 | 119.3947 | -19.4572 | 0.9199 |
| | a1 | 349.2082 | -3.4200 | -0.0013 | 348.1896 | -0.4974 | 0.0063 | 348.1582 | 2.1950 | 0.0100 |
| | a2 | -0.1452 | 0.3177 | | -0.0781 | 0.4961 | | 0.0656 | 0.4482 | |
| 3 | a0 | 129.3532 | -16.7745 | 0.9013 | 113.3304 | -21.6032 | 0.9089 | 107.6182 | -16.8152 | 0.9299 |
| | a1 | 348.9956 | -2.7838 | 0.0011 | 348.0343 | 0.4978 | 0.0089 | 348.2948 | 3.0934 | 0.0121 |
| | a2 | -0.1699 | 0.3785 | | -0.0304 | 0.5046 | | 0.0507 | 0.3948 | |
| 4 | a0 | 118.1788 | -19.1786 | 0.9025 | 101.3350 | -20.6010 | 0.9202 | 95.9627 | -13.3284 | 0.9420 |
| | a1 | 348.6522 | -2.0256 | 0.0038 | 347.9765 | 1.5101 | 0.0115 | 348.4010 | 3.8853 | 0.0139 |
| | a2 | -0.1709 | 0.4335 | | 0.0044 | 0.4927 | | 0.0007 | 0.3267 | |
| 5 | a0 | 106.6605 | -20.7697 | 0.9064 | 89.3161 | -18.5989 | 0.9317 | 84.3628 | -11.1182 | 0.9560 |
| | a1 | 348.3071 | -1.1569 | 0.0066 | 347.9895 | 2.4984 | 0.0138 | 348.4060 | 4.5414 | 0.0152 |
| | a2 | -0.1481 | 0.4794 | | 0.0146 | 0.4599 | | -0.0007 | 0.2409 | |
| 6 | a0 | 94.8204 | -21.4466 | 0.9130 | 77.3198 | -15.6417 | 0.9454 | 72.6884 | -4.3382 | 0.9712 |
| | a1 | 348.0090 | -0.1956 | 0.0094 | 348.0232 | 3.4216 | 0.0155 | 348.2512 | 5.0273 | 0.0155 |
| | a2 | -0.1069 | 0.5109 | | -0.0055 | 0.1584 | | -0.1774 | 0.1310 | |
| 7 | a0 | 82.7234 | -21.1310 | 0.9224 | 65.3366 | -11.8167 | 0.9610 | 60.7601 | 2.8172 | 0.9868 |
| | a1 | 347.7954 | 0.8996 | 0.0119 | 348.0162 | 4.2359 | 0.0163 | 347.8959 | 5.2943 | 0.0146 |
| | a2 | -0.0591 | 0.5224 | | -0.0549 | 0.3250 | | -0.2824 | -0.0113 | |
| 8 | a0 | 70.4605 | -19.7793 | 0.9344 | 53.2965 | -7.2580 | 0.9774 | 48.3717 | 6.0965 | 1.0015 |
| | a1 | 347.6796 | 1.8785 | 0.0139 | 347.9090 | 4.8908 | 0.0159 | 347.3263 | 5.2766 | 0.0121 |
| | a2 | -0.0195 | 0.5085 | | -0.1272 | 0.2138 | | -0.3709 | -0.1898 | |
| 9 | a0 | 58.1209 | -17.3933 | 0.9483 | 41.0765 | -2.1566 | 0.9934 | 35.3264 | 11.1791 | 1.0137 |
| | a1 | 347.6444 | 2.9000 | 0.0151 | 347.6549 | 5.3236 | 0.0139 | 346.5737 | 4.8993 | 0.0081 |
| | a2 | -0.0014 | 0.4647 | | -0.2107 | 0.0662 | | -0.4075 | -0.3954 | |
| 10 | a0 | 45.7637 | -14.0302 | 0.9635 | 28.5192 | 3.2294 | 1.0074 | 21.4938 | 15.6788 | 1.0218 |
| | a1 | 347.6459 | 3.8344 | 0.0152 | 347.2304 | 5.4605 | 0.0103 | 345.7425 | 4.1045 | 0.0029 |
| | a2 | -0.0116 | 0.3876 | | -0.2862 | -0.1175 | | -0.3503 | -0.5979 | |
| 11 | a0 | 33.3927 | -9.8105 | 0.9787 | 15.4626 | 8.5681 | 1.0177 | 6.8895 | 19.1824 | 1.0247 |
| | a1 | 347.6263 | 4.6147 | 0.0139 | 346.6501 | 5.2271 | 0.0054 | 345.0260 | 2.8969 | -0.0029 |
| | a2 | -0.0495 | 0.2752 | | -0.3251 | -0.3252 | | -0.1782 | -0.7478 | |
| 12 | a0 | 20.9729 | -4.9237 | 0.9927 | 1.7882 | 13.4658 | 1.0232 | 351.7425 | 21.3304 | 1.0218 |
| | a1 | 347.5293 | 5.1698 | 0.0112 | 345.9874 | 4.5730 | -0.0002 | 344.6640 | 1.3845 | -0.0083 |
| | a2 | -0.1071 | 0.1280 | | -0.2937 | -0.5282 | | 0.0734 | -0.7981 | |
| 13 | a0 | 8.3938 | 0.3705 | 1.0040 | 345.4844 | 17.5074 | 1.0229 | 336.4847 | 21.9181 | 1.0134 |
| | a1 | 347.3144 | 5.4094 | 0.0074 | 345.3867 | 3.5065 | -0.0056 | 344.8196 | -0.2065 | -0.0126 |
| | a2 | -0.1702 | -0.0481 | | -0.1704 | -0.6853 | | 0.3150 | -0.7367 | |
| 14 | a0 | 355.5370 | 5.7474 | 1.0113 | 332.7047 | 20.3271 | 1.0172 | 321.6225 | 20.9578 | 1.0008 |
| | a1 | 346.9700 | 5.3335 | 0.0028 | 345.0387 | 2.1217 | -0.0102 | 345.4668 | -1.7075 | -0.0153 |
| | a2 | -0.2179 | -0.2399 | | 0.0273 | -0.7580 | | 0.1646 | -0.5957 | |
| 15 | a0 | 342.2890 | 10.8372 | 1.0141 | 317.7750 | 21.6913 | 1.0069 | 307.5547 | 18.6581 | 0.9854 |
| | a1 | 346.5265 | 4.8372 | -0.0019 | 345.0971 | 0.5921 | -0.0133 | 346.4116 | -2.8994 | -0.0164 |
| | a2 | -0.2256 | -0.4261 | | 0.2375 | -0.7333 | | 0.4992 | -0.4265 | |

$$GHA°,\ DEC° = (a_2x + a_1)x + a_0 \qquad HP° = a_1x + a_0 \qquad \text{where } x = GMT^h/24$$

---

## Table 1: SUN AND PLANETS, 1981

| | September GHA-GMT (h) | September DEC (°) | October GHA-GMT (h) | October DEC (°) | November GHA-GMT (h) | November DEC (°) | December GHA-GMT (h) | December DEC (°) |
|---|---|---|---|---|---|---|---|---|
| **Sun** a0 | 11.99282 | 8.7565 | 12.16419 | -2.6764 | 12.27219 | -14.0072 | 12.19132 | -21.5940 |
| a1 | 0.16300 | -11.5176 | 0.17333 | -12.1465 | 0.02197 | -10.4174 | -0.19238 | -5.2681 |
| a2 | 0.05271 | -1.1644 | -0.02931 | 0.2626 | -0.00272 | 1.9235 | -0.09039 | 3.5141 |
| a3 | -0.03496 | 0.4529 | -0.00254 | 0.4928 | -0.02990 | 0.6178 | 0.02644 | 0.4624 |
| a4 | 0.00133 | 0.0194 | 0.00710 | 0.0356 | 0.01741 | -0.0262 | 0.01015 | -0.1598 |
| check sum | 12.17490 | -3.4532 | 12.27277 | -14.3309 | 12.17895 | -21.9095 | 11.94514 | -23.0454 |
| **Venus** a0 | 9.69550 | -5.6712 | 9.45611 | -19.3293 | 9.04641 | -26.5930 | 8.87676 | -24.4064 |
| a1 | -0.19063 | -16.2894 | -0.35179 | -11.9365 | -0.42538 | -2.4724 | 0.21447 | 6.4137 |
| a2 | -0.02160 | -0.3285 | -0.11278 | 3.7060 | 0.14185 | 5.5435 | 0.59659 | 3.2525 |
| a3 | -0.06539 | 1.0587 | 0.00704 | 1.1748 | 0.01514 | -0.0694 | 0.23870 | -1.5674 |
| a4 | 0.01579 | -0.0158 | 0.03463 | -0.2797 | 0.01514 | -0.4020 | 0.03408 | -0.2605 |
| check sum | 9.43367 | -20.0607 | 9.03321 | -26.6647 | 8.89251 | -23.9933 | 9.96060 | -16.5681 |
| **Mars** a0 | 14.53854 | 21.3437 | 15.22722 | 16.8047 | 16.07244 | 8.0685 | 17.01843 | 4.8945 |
| a1 | 0.66681 | -3.8645 | 0.77244 | -5.6527 | 0.92447 | -3.6248 | 1.08065 | -6.1527 |
| a2 | 0.07329 | -1.2125 | 0.07687 | -0.6638 | 0.07328 | -0.1057 | 0.08368 | 0.4219 |
| a3 | 0.00250 | 0.1720 | -0.00819 | 0.1679 | -0.00618 | 0.1558 | 0.00321 | 0.1584 |
| a4 | 0.00154 | 0.0102 | 0.00359 | 0.0116 | 0.00055 | 0.0179 | 0.00828 | 0.0257 |
| check sum | 15.27768 | 16.4489 | 16.07193 | 10.6677 | 17.08630 | 4.5117 | 18.19425 | -0.6522 |
| **Jupiter** a0 | 9.87292 | 3.4991 | 11.46210 | -5.9295 | 13.08129 | -8.4429 | 14.66189 | -10.6284 |
| a1 | 1.71833 | -2.5051 | 1.67718 | -2.6408 | 1.67173 | -2.5051 | 1.70744 | -2.2191 |
| a2 | -0.03041 | -0.1446 | -0.01148 | 0.0045 | 0.00882 | 0.1480 | 0.03230 | 0.2743 |
| a3 | 0.00598 | 0.0510 | 0.00489 | 0.0428 | 0.00537 | 0.0362 | 0.00764 | 0.0330 |
| a4 | 0.00007 | -0.0010 | 0.00085 | 0.0020 | 0.00152 | 0.0040 | 0.00151 | 0.0036 |
| check sum | 11.56689 | -6.0946 | 13.13354 | -8.5210 | 14.76873 | -10.7598 | 16.41078 | -12.4366 |
| **Saturn** a0 | 10.02447 | -1.3282 | 11.77899 | -2.7361 | 13.58380 | -4.1671 | 15.35431 | -5.3269 |
| a1 | 1.88591 | -1.4433 | 1.86173 | -1.5270 | 1.87004 | -1.3914 | 1.91283 | -0.1502 |
| a2 | -0.02039 | -0.0981 | -0.00393 | 0.0160 | 0.01416 | 0.1319 | 0.03247 | 0.2352 |
| a3 | 0.00508 | 0.0374 | 0.00495 | 0.0346 | 0.00534 | 0.0329 | 0.00592 | 0.0310 |
| a4 | 0.00022 | 0.0006 | 0.00055 | 0.0021 | 0.00065 | 0.0021 | 0.00012 | -0.0009 |
| check sum | 11.89529 | -2.8316 | 13.64225 | -4.2104 | 15.47399 | -5.3916 | 17.30565 | -6.1118 |

**Semi-diameter of the Sun**

| | | |
|---|---|---|
| Sept 1 - Sept 14 | 0.265 | |
| Sept 15 - Sept 28 | 0.266 | |
| Sept 29 - Oct 11 | 0.267 | |
| Oct 12 - Oct 24 | 0.268 | |
| Oct 25 - Nov 7 | 0.269 | |
| Nov 8 - Nov 25 | 0.270 | |
| Nov 26 - Dec 28 | 0.271 | |
| Dec 29 - Dec 31 | 0.272 | |

**Parallax of Venus (HP)**

| | |
|---|---|
| Sept 1 - Sept 30 | 0.002 |
| Oct 1 - Nov 6 | 0.003 |
| Nov 7 - Nov 27 | 0.004 |
| Nov 28 - Dec 11 | 0.005 |
| Dec 12 - Dec 21 | 0.006 |
| Dec 22 - Dec 30 | 0.007 |
| Dec 31 | 0.008 |

**Parallax of Mars (HP)**

| | |
|---|---|
| Sept 1 - Nov 26 | 0.001 |
| Nov 27 - Dec 31 | 0.002 |

$$GHA° = 15(((((a_4x + a_3)x + a_2)x + a_1)x + a_0)x + GMT^h)$$

$$DEC° = (((a_4x + a_3)x + a_2)x + a_1)x + a_0$$

$$\text{where } x = (d + GMT^h/24)/32$$

## Table 5: APPARENT PLACES OF STARS, 1981

### SHA (Sidereal Hour Angle)

| Mag | No | Name | $a_0$ (°) | Jan | Feb | Mar | Apr | May | Jun | Jul | Aug | Sep | Oct | Nov | Dec |
|---|---|---|---|---|---|---|---|---|---|---|---|---|---|---|---|
| 2.2 | 1 | Alpheratz α And | 358.1334 | 160 | 180 | 182 | 188 | 159 | 123 | 83 | 45 | 16 | 0 | 0 | 13 |
| 2.4 | 2 | Ankaa α Phe | 353.6477 | 174 | 199 | 211 | 207 | 186 | 149 | 105 | 58 | 20 | 0 | 0 | 17 |
| 2.5 | 3 | Schedar α Cas | 350.1235 | 189 | 229 | 254 | 257 | 234 | 187 | 130 | 73 | 28 | 3 | 0 | 20 |
| 2.2 | 4 | Diphda β Cet | 349.3260 | 155 | 173 | 182 | 179 | 163 | 133 | 97 | 58 | 25 | 5 | 0 | 14 |
| 0.6 | 5 | Achernar α Eri | 335.7308 | 160 | 203 | 235 | 252 | 245 | 214 | 166 | 106 | 49 | 11 | 0 | 17 |
| 2.2 | 6 | Hamal α Ari | 328.4577 | 150 | 170 | 187 | 195 | 188 | 165 | 131 | 90 | 51 | 20 | 2 | 13 |
| 3.1 | 7 | Acamar θ Eri | 315.5993 | 117 | 145 | 170 | 191 | 196 | 184 | 155 | 113 | 66 | 27 | 3 | 9 |
| 2.8 | 8 | Menkar α Cet | 314.6620 | 137 | 153 | 170 | 182 | 182 | 168 | 141 | 105 | 66 | 32 | 8 | 8 |
| 1.9 | 9 | Mirfak α Per | 309.2365 | 178 | 205 | 238 | 260 | 267 | 251 | 213 | 158 | 99 | 46 | 12 | 14 |
| 1.1 | 10 | Aldebaran α Tau | 291.2744 | 137 | 147 | 164 | 183 | 193 | 189 | 170 | 137 | 97 | 56 | 21 | 2 |
| 0.3 | 11 | Rigel β Ori | 281.5774 | 113 | 121 | 137 | 157 | 171 | 173 | 161 | 135 | 98 | 59 | 23 | 2 |
| 0.2 | 12 | Capella α Aur | 281.1561 | 166 | 176 | 200 | 229 | 251 | 252 | 232 | 192 | 140 | 86 | 35 | 3 |
| 1.7 | 13 | Bellatrix γ Ori | 278.9548 | 123 | 129 | 144 | 163 | 178 | 178 | 166 | 140 | 103 | 63 | 26 | 3 |
| 1.8 | 14 | Elnath β Tau | 278.7080 | 143 | 148 | 165 | 187 | 202 | 204 | 190 | 159 | 117 | 72 | 30 | 3 |
| 1.8 | 15 | Alnilam ε Ori | 276.1710 | 116 | 121 | 135 | 155 | 169 | 173 | 163 | 138 | 103 | 63 | 26 | 4 |
| 0-1 | 16 | Betelgeuse α Ori | 271.4470 | 120 | 123 | 136 | 155 | 170 | 175 | 167 | 143 | 108 | 68 | 29 | 4 |
| -0.9 | 17 | Canopus α Car | 264.1015 | 45 | 59 | 89 | 132 | 167 | 197 | 203 | 185 | 145 | 92 | 37 | 4 |
| -1.6 | 18 | Sirius α CMa | 258.9072 | 83 | 93 | 105 | 126 | 145 | 158 | 157 | 140 | 110 | 72 | 31 | 4 |
| 1.6 | 19 | Adhara ε CMa | 255.5150 | 79 | 79 | 92 | 116 | 139 | 156 | 159 | 146 | 117 | 77 | 34 | 4 |
| 0.5 | 20 | Procyon α CMi | 245.4074 | 105 | 95 | 100 | 115 | 134 | 148 | 150 | 138 | 112 | 77 | 36 | 5 |
| 1.2 | 21 | Pollux β Gem | 243.9443 | 122 | 109 | 113 | 130 | 150 | 169 | 175 | 167 | 145 | 110 | 64 | 15 |
| 1.7 | 22 | Avior ε Car | 234.4539 | 0 | 17 | 57 | 105 | 152 | 184 | 192 | 173 | 123 | 64 | 18 | 2 |
| 2.2 | 23 | Suhail λ Vel | 223.1626 | 53 | 31 | 32 | 50 | 77 | 106 | 128 | 136 | 124 | 93 | 47 | 5 |
| 1.8 | 24 | Miaplacidus β Car | 221.7287 | 28 | 0 | 13 | 62 | 131 | 207 | 267 | 301 | 293 | 242 | 160 | 76 |
| 2.2 | 25 | Alphard α Hya | 218.3235 | 87 | 65 | 59 | 65 | 80 | 98 | 110 | 112 | 100 | 75 | 39 | 6 |
| 1.3 | 26 | Regulus α Leo | 208.1474 | 95 | 67 | 54 | 55 | 67 | 84 | 98 | 103 | 94 | 73 | 39 | 5 |
| 2.0 | 27 | Dubhe α UMa | 194.3482 | 98 | 36 | 3 | 0 | 25 | 68 | 109 | 137 | 141 | 120 | 73 | 20 |
| 2.2 | 28 | Denebola β Leo | 182.9678 | 89 | 52 | 28 | 16 | 18 | 31 | 48 | 61 | 65 | 57 | 34 | 6 |
| 2.8 | 29 | Gienah γ Crv | 176.2838 | 86 | 48 | 22 | 6 | 6 | 16 | 32 | 48 | 57 | 53 | 32 | 4 |
| 1.1 | 30 | Acrux α Cru | 173.5987 | 136 | 67 | 23 | 0 | 6 | 36 | 80 | 128 | 163 | 168 | 139 | 83 |

### DEC (Declination)

| Mag | No | Name | $a_0$ (°) | Jan | Feb | Mar | Apr | May | Jun | Jul | Aug | Sep | Oct | Nov | Dec |
|---|---|---|---|---|---|---|---|---|---|---|---|---|---|---|---|
| 2.2 | 1 | Alpheratz α And | N 28.9825 | 41 | 30 | 18 | 9 | 4 | 8 | 18 | 38 | 59 | 77 | 90 | 96 |
| 2.4 | 2 | Ankaa α Phe | S 42.4034 | 115 | 111 | 97 | 75 | 50 | 25 | 8 | 5 | 20 | 40 | 40 | 56 |
| 2.5 | 3 | Schedar α Cas | N 56.4292 | 71 | 63 | 46 | 25 | 8 | 0 | 6 | 23 | 48 | 75 | 100 | 117 |
| 2.2 | 4 | Diphda β Cet | S 18.0859 | 87 | 89 | 85 | 74 | 57 | 37 | 19 | 5 | 0 | 4 | 14 | 25 |
| 0.6 | 5 | Achernar α Eri | S 57.3267 | 132 | 131 | 118 | 93 | 63 | 34 | 11 | 0 | 21 | 46 | 46 | 68 |
| 2.2 | 6 | Hamal α Ari | N 23.3705 | 22 | 18 | 12 | 4 | 1 | 2 | 12 | 25 | 40 | 53 | 63 | 69 |
| 3.1 | 7 | Acamar θ Eri | S 40.3748 | 111 | 120 | 117 | 102 | 79 | 51 | 26 | 6 | 0 | 6 | 21 | 49 |
| 2.8 | 8 | Menkar α Cet | N 4.0127 | 4 | 2 | 0 | 0 | 0 | 5 | 14 | 26 | 41 | 56 | 61 | 56 |
| 1.9 | 9 | Mirfak α Per | N 49.7913 | 44 | 47 | 33 | 19 | 6 | 0 | 3 | 13 | 28 | 47 | 65 | — |
| 1.1 | 10 | Aldebaran α Tau | N 16.4698 | 5 | 3 | 2 | 0 | 2 | 8 | 17 | 25 | 30 | 32 | — | — |
| 0.3 | 11 | Rigel β Ori | S 8.2203 | 52 | 63 | 68 | 67 | 60 | 47 | 31 | 15 | 3 | 0 | 7 | 20 |
| 0.2 | 12 | Capella α Aur | N 45.9771 | 21 | 32 | 37 | 35 | 27 | 16 | 6 | 0 | 4 | 12 | 23 | — |
| 1.7 | 13 | Bellatrix γ Ori | N 6.3303 | 9 | 5 | 3 | 1 | 3 | 10 | 19 | 30 | 39 | 42 | 39 | 32 |
| 1.8 | 14 | Elnath β Tau | N 28.5907 | 3 | 7 | 9 | 8 | 5 | 2 | 2 | 8 | 17 | 25 | 30 | — |
| 1.8 | 15 | Alnilam ε Ori | S 1.2115 | 40 | 50 | 54 | 54 | 49 | 39 | 27 | 13 | 3 | 0 | 7 | 15 |
| 0-1 | 16 | Betelgeuse α Ori | N 7.4015 | 9 | 5 | 3 | 1 | 3 | 9 | 17 | 26 | 34 | 36 | 32 | 25 |
| -0.9 | 17 | Canopus α Car | S 52.6806 | 64 | 91 | 107 | 112 | 103 | 82 | 56 | 28 | 7 | 0 | 2 | 33 |
| -1.6 | 18 | Sirius α CMa | S 16.6879 | 38 | 57 | 67 | 70 | 65 | 52 | 36 | 18 | 4 | 0 | 7 | 24 |
| 1.6 | 19 | Adhara ε CMa | S 28.9426 | 44 | 67 | 81 | 87 | 82 | 67 | 47 | 25 | 6 | 0 | 4 | 25 |
| 0.5 | 20 | Procyon α CMi | N 5.2716 | 14 | 8 | 5 | 1 | 0 | 6 | 15 | 27 | 27 | 27 | — | — |
| 1.2 | 21 | Pollux β Gem | N 28.0694 | 15 | 18 | 23 | 23 | 20 | 13 | 6 | 0 | 4 | 12 | 23 | — |
| 1.7 | 22 | Avior ε Car | S 59.4449 | 18 | 50 | 75 | 90 | 90 | 71 | 45 | 19 | 2 | 0 | 5 | 19 |
| 2.2 | 23 | Suhail λ Vel | S 43.3531 | 33 | 57 | 76 | 83 | 78 | 64 | 42 | 19 | 5 | 0 | 4 | 18 |
| 1.8 | 24 | Miaplacidus β Car | S 69.6357 | 32 | 61 | 86 | 98 | 97 | 83 | 59 | 31 | 10 | 0 | 3 | 18 |
| 2.2 | 25 | Alphard α Hya | S 8.5755 | 19 | 31 | 38 | 38 | 33 | 24 | 13 | 4 | 0 | 2 | 15 | — |
| 1.3 | 26 | Regulus α Leo | N 12.0568 | 28 | 18 | 15 | 17 | 23 | 29 | 33 | 34 | 27 | 15 | — | — |
| 2.0 | 27 | Dubhe α UMa | N 61.8457 | 41 | 48 | 64 | 87 | 106 | 116 | 113 | 98 | 74 | 47 | 20 | — |
| 2.2 | 28 | Denebola β Leo | N 14.6744 | 34 | 21 | 18 | 21 | 29 | 38 | 43 | 45 | 42 | 33 | 18 | — |
| 2.8 | 29 | Gienah γ Crv | S 17.4336 | 0 | 20 | 36 | 49 | 56 | 57 | 53 | 46 | 36 | 29 | 28 | 36 |
| 1.1 | 30 | Acrux α Cru | S 62.9875 | 20 | 45 | 75 | 101 | 118 | 124 | 117 | 99 | 77 | 56 | 47 | — |

## Table 5: APPARENT PLACES OF STARS, 1981

### DEC (Declination)

| Mag | No | Name | | a₀ (°) | Jan | Feb | Mar | Apr | May | Jun | Jul | Aug | Sep | Oct | Nov | Dec |
|---|---|---|---|---|---|---|---|---|---|---|---|---|---|---|---|---|
| 1.6 | 31 | Gacrux | γ Cru | S 57.0007 | +0.6 | +0.9 | +0.9 | +0.8 | +0.5 | +0.2 | -0.2 | -0.6 | -0.6 | -0.2 | +0.2 | +0.2 |
| 1.7 | 32 | Alioth | ε UMa | N 56.0565 | -0.2 | +0.3 | +0.6 | +0.8 | +0.6 | +0.3 | -0.1 | -0.5 | -0.8 | -1.0 | -1.0 | -0.7 |
| 1.2 | 33 | Spica | α Vir | S 11.0598 | +0.1 | +0.1 | +0.1 | +0.1 | 0.0 | -0.1 | -0.1 | 0.0 | +0.1 | +0.2 | +0.3 | +0.5 |
| 1.9 | 34 | Alkaid | η UMa | N 49.4031 | -0.4 | +0.3 | +0.7 | +0.8 | +0.7 | +0.4 | -0.1 | -0.5 | -0.8 | -1.0 | -1.0 | -0.8 |
| 0.9 | 35 | Hadar | β Cen | S 60.2754 | +0.4 | +0.6 | +0.8 | +0.8 | +0.6 | +0.3 | 0.0 | -0.2 | -0.3 | -0.6 | -0.7 | -0.8 |
| 2.3 | 36 | Menkent | θ Cen | S 36.2721 | +0.4 | +0.5 | +0.6 | +0.5 | +0.4 | +0.2 | 0.0 | -0.2 | -0.3 | -0.4 | -0.5 | -0.4 |
| 0.2 | 37 | Arcturus | α Boo | N 19.2780 | -0.6 | -0.2 | +0.1 | +0.2 | +0.1 | +0.1 | 0.0 | 0.0 | +0.1 | +0.2 | +0.1 | -0.2 |
| 0.1 | 38 | Rigil Kentaurus | α Cen | S 60.7501 | +0.2 | +0.5 | +0.7 | +0.7 | +0.6 | +0.4 | +0.1 | -0.2 | -0.5 | -0.7 | -0.8 | -0.8 |
| 2.9 | 39 | Zubenelgenubi | α Lib | S 15.9603 | +0.4 | +0.4 | +0.3 | +0.2 | 0.0 | -0.1 | -0.1 | -0.1 | -0.1 | +0.1 | +0.3 | +0.3 |
| 2.2 | 40 | Kochab | β UMi | N 74.2292 | -0.5 | 0.0 | +0.6 | +0.8 | +0.8 | +0.6 | +0.2 | -0.3 | -0.8 | -1.1 | -1.1 | -0.9 |
| 2.3 | 41 | Alphecca | α CrB | N 26.7753 | -0.6 | -0.3 | +0.1 | +0.5 | +0.5 | +0.3 | +0.1 | -0.1 | -0.5 | -0.8 | -1.1 | -0.9 |
| 1.2 | 42 | Antares | α Sco | S 26.3876 | +0.2 | +0.2 | +0.2 | +0.1 | 0.0 | -0.1 | -0.1 | +0.1 | +0.2 | +0.2 | +0.1 | +0.1 |
| 1.9 | 43 | Atria | α TrA | S 68.9889 | +0.1 | +0.4 | +0.6 | +0.7 | +0.6 | +0.4 | +0.1 | -0.2 | -0.5 | -0.7 | -0.7 | -0.6 |
| 2.6 | 44 | Sabik | η Oph | S 15.7001 | 0.0 | +0.7 | +0.4 | +0.3 | +0.2 | +0.1 | 0.0 | 0.0 | +0.1 | +0.1 | 0.0 | -0.2 |
| 1.7 | 45 | Shaula | λ Sco | S 37.0882 | -0.1 | -0.1 | 0.0 | +0.3 | +0.2 | +0.2 | +0.1 | +0.2 | +0.3 | +0.3 | +0.1 | -0.2 |
| 2.1 | 46 | Rasalhague | α Oph | N 12.5712 | -0.6 | -0.3 | 0.0 | +0.1 | +0.2 | +0.1 | 0.0 | 0.0 | -0.1 | -0.2 | -0.2 | -0.2 |
| 2.4 | 47 | Eltanin | γ Dra | N 51.4867 | -0.6 | -0.2 | +0.3 | +0.5 | +0.6 | +0.5 | +0.3 | +0.1 | -0.3 | -0.7 | -1.0 | -1.0 |
| 2.0 | 48 | Kaus Australis | ε Sgr | S 34.3924 | -0.9 | -0.4 | 0.0 | +0.2 | +0.5 | +0.6 | +0.5 | +0.4 | +0.3 | -0.2 | -0.7 | -1.0 |
| 0.1 | 49 | Vega | α Lyr | N 38.7617 | -0.9 | -0.6 | -0.2 | +0.3 | +0.5 | +0.5 | +0.2 | -0.2 | -0.6 | -0.9 | -0.9 | -0.8 |
| 2.1 | 50 | Nunki | σ Sgr | S 26.3191 | -0.9 | -0.6 | -0.2 | +0.1 | +0.4 | +0.6 | +0.7 | +0.6 | +0.2 | -0.2 | -0.6 | -0.9 |
| 0.9 | 51 | Altair | α Aql | N 8.8156 | -0.7 | -0.4 | -0.1 | +0.2 | +0.5 | +0.6 | +0.5 | +0.2 | -0.1 | -0.3 | -0.4 | -0.4 |
| 2.1 | 52 | Peacock | α Pav | S 56.7922 | -0.7 | -0.3 | +0.2 | +0.5 | +0.6 | +0.7 | +0.5 | +0.3 | -0.1 | -0.4 | -0.6 | -0.7 |
| 1.3 | 53 | Deneb | α Cyg | N 45.2081 | -0.5 | -0.1 | +0.2 | +0.5 | +0.7 | +0.7 | +0.5 | +0.1 | -0.2 | -0.5 | -0.6 | -0.6 |
| 2.5 | 54 | Enif | ε Peg | N 9.7852 | -0.4 | -0.3 | -0.1 | +0.1 | +0.5 | +0.7 | +0.8 | +0.7 | +0.4 | -0.1 | -0.2 | -0.3 |
| 2.2 | 55 | Al Na'ir | α Gru | S 47.0483 | -0.4 | -0.1 | +0.2 | +0.6 | +0.8 | +0.8 | +0.7 | +0.5 | +0.1 | -0.3 | -0.5 | -0.3 |
| 1.3 | 56 | Fomalhaut | α PsA | S 29.7183 | -0.2 | -0.4 | -0.5 | -0.6 | -0.2 | +0.2 | +0.5 | +0.7 | +0.3 | +0.1 | +0.2 | +0.1 |
| 2.6 | 57 | Markab | α Peg | N 15.1002 | -0.4 | -0.2 | 0.0 | +0.2 | +0.5 | +0.6 | +0.5 | +0.5 | +0.5 | +0.1 | 0.0 | +0.7 |
| | | | | | | | | | p (Polar Distance) | | | | | | | |
| 2.1 | 58 | Polaris | | 0.8165 | 24 | 16 | 23 | 44 | 69 | 92 | 103 | 102 | 86 | 62 | 30 | 0 |
| 5.5 | 59 | σ Octantis | | 0.9659 | 0 | 30 | 57 | 81 | 93 | 92 | 80 | 57 | 30 | 9 | -1.0 | +0.7 |

### SHA (Sidereal Hour Angle)

| Mag | No | Name | | a₀ | Jan | Feb | Mar | Apr | May | Jun | Jul | Aug | Sep | Oct | Nov | Dec |
|---|---|---|---|---|---|---|---|---|---|---|---|---|---|---|---|---|
| 1.6 | 31 | Gacrux | γ Cru | 172.4593 | 121 | 62 | 22 | -2 | 25 | 59 | 98 | 125 | 129 | 104 | 56 | -2.6 |
| 1.7 | 32 | Alioth | ε UMa | 166.6905 | 136 | 75 | 28 | 0 | 2 | 25 | 59 | 94 | 119 | 126 | 111 | 73 |
| 1.2 | 33 | Spica | α Vir | 158.9431 | 106 | 66 | 34 | 10 | 0 | 3 | 16 | 32 | 46 | 49 | 38 | 13 |
| 1.9 | 34 | Alkaid | η UMa | 153.2914 | 145 | 91 | 46 | 11 | 0 | 11 | 36 | 68 | 96 | 110 | 107 | 83 |
| 0.9 | 35 | Hadar | β Cen | 149.3651 | 200 | 128 | 69 | 22 | 0 | 9 | 37 | 71 | 113 | 137 | 133 | 97 |
| 2.3 | 36 | Menkent | θ Cen | 148.5986 | 139 | 91 | 51 | 18 | 1 | 0 | 13 | 34 | 56 | 67 | 62 | 38 |
| 0.2 | 37 | Arcturus | α Boo | 146.2924 | 121 | 81 | 45 | 15 | 0 | 0 | 12 | 30 | 48 | 57 | 55 | 37 |
| 0.1 | 38 | Rigil Kentaurus | α Cen | 140.4066 | 216 | 144 | 82 | 29 | 1 | 0 | 23 | 64 | 109 | 140 | 140 | 116 |
| 2.9 | 39 | Zubenelgenubi | α Lib | 137.5332 | 140 | 100 | 62 | 28 | 7 | 0 | 8 | 25 | 45 | 59 | 59 | 55 |
| 2.2 | 40 | Kochab | β UMi | 137.2935 | 332 | 227 | 136 | 37 | 0 | 6 | 45 | 124 | 215 | 272 | 346 | 377 |
| 2.3 | 41 | Alphecca | α CrB | 126.5190 | -12 | -13 | -12 | -9 | -6 | -3 | 0 | 24 | 45 | 64 | 73 | 66 |
| 1.2 | 42 | Antares | α Sco | 112.9276 | 183 | 145 | 105 | 60 | 26 | 5 | 0 | 28 | 86 | 148 | 193 | 198 |
| 1.9 | 43 | Atria | α TrA | 108.3148 | 408 | 328 | 237 | 137 | 59 | 10 | 0 | 28 | 86 | 148 | 193 | 198 |
| 2.6 | 44 | Sabik | η Oph | 102.6662 | 181 | 149 | 112 | 69 | 34 | 9 | 0 | 5 | 20 | 39 | 53 | 54 |
| 1.7 | 45 | Shaula | λ Sco | 96.9067 | 220 | 185 | 142 | 91 | 47 | 15 | 0 | 3 | 21 | 44 | 64 | 69 |
| 2.1 | 46 | Rasalhague | α Oph | 96.4756 | 171 | 144 | 110 | 69 | 34 | 9 | 0 | 5 | 20 | 40 | 57 | 63 |
| 2.4 | 47 | Eltanin | γ Dra | 90.9454 | 212 | 186 | 143 | 88 | 40 | 10 | 0 | 15 | 47 | 86 | 124 | 148 |
| 2.0 | 48 | Kaus Australis | ε Sgr | 84.2581 | 223 | 195 | 157 | 108 | 62 | 25 | 4 | 0 | 12 | 34 | 56 | 66 |
| 0.1 | 49 | Vega | α Lyr | 80.9136 | 189 | 171 | 138 | 92 | 48 | 15 | 0 | 3 | 22 | 49 | 78 | 99 |
| 2.1 | 50 | Nunki | σ Sgr | 76.4645 | 210 | 189 | 156 | 112 | 68 | 31 | 8 | 0 | 8 | 26 | 47 | 59 |
| 0.9 | 51 | Altair | α Aql | 62.5233 | 180 | 170 | 147 | 110 | 71 | 35 | 11 | 0 | 3 | 17 | 37 | 53 |
| 2.1 | 52 | Peacock | α Pav | 53.9436 | 312 | 301 | 267 | 209 | 144 | 80 | 30 | 1 | 0 | 23 | 64 | 96 |
| 1.3 | 53 | Deneb | α Cyg | 49.7896 | -94 | -97 | -92 | -42 | -95 | -1 | 12 | 48 | 92 | 109 | 110 | 110 |
| 2.5 | 54 | Enif | ε Peg | 34.1734 | 173 | 167 | 147 | 107 | 68 | 35 | 11 | 0 | 5 | 18 | 35 | 35 |
| 2.2 | 55 | Al Na'ir | α Gru | 28.2235 | 238 | 247 | 237 | 205 | 161 | 108 | 59 | 20 | 0 | 6 | 23 | 52 |
| 1.3 | 56 | Fomalhaut | α PsA | 15.8343 | 90 | 201 | 199 | 180 | 148 | 107 | 66 | 30 | 6 | 0 | 9 | 28 |
| 2.6 | 57 | Markab | α Peg | 14.0322 | 164 | 177 | 177 | 161 | 133 | 96 | 59 | 27 | 7 | 0 | 7 | 23 |
| | | | | | | | | | | SHA/s | | | | | | |
| 2.1 | 58 | Polaris | | 4.6610 | 48 | 75 | 99 | 116 | 119 | 107 | 84 | 55 | 29 | 10 | 0 | -0.6 |
| 5.5 | 59 | σ Octantis | | 0.7830 | 128 | 130 | 119 | 96 | 67 | 37 | 14 | 0 | 1 | 17 | 42 | 66 |

# Appendix C
# Answers to Exercises

All intermediate results are rounded to four places of decimals; but final answers are given to the nearest minute. Due to this rounding, the last two decimal places may well be different from your own calculator results. No notice should be taken of such differences as they have no significant effect on the final answer.

**Exercise 1** (Chapter 3)

| 1 | d.Lat | 98.4808′ |
|---|---|---|
| | departure | −17.3648 miles |
| | d.Long | −0°.3370 |
| | EP'Lat | 31°.6413 |
| | EP Long | −15°.3370 |

     *EP    31° 38.5′N  15° 20′W*

| 2 | d.Lat | −154.2690′ |
|---|---|---|
| | departure | 183.8507 miles |
| | d.Long | 3°.0644 |
| | EP Lat | −0°.5378 |
| | EP Long | 48°.4811 |

     *EP    0° 32′S  48° 29′E*

| 3 | d.Lat | −349.8479′ |
|---|---|---|
| | departure | −193.9238 miles |
| | d.Long | −3°.2323 |
| | EP Lat | −2°.1641 |
| | EP Long | 2°.9343 |

     *EP    2° 10′S  2° 56′E*

| 4 | d.Lat | −22.7236′ |
|---|---|---|
| | departure | 10.5158 miles |
| | d.Long | 0°.2794 |
| | EP Lat | 50°.9546 |
| | EP Long | 1°.8460 |

     *EP    50° 57′N  1° 51′E*

5    d.Lat              −49.2503′

| 5 | d.Lat | −49.2503′ |
|---|-------|-----------|
| | departure | −52.6002 miles |
| | d.Long | −1°.4798 |
| | EP Lat | 53°.2592 |
| | EP Long | 3°.4986 |

*EP*    *53° 15.5′ N   3° 30′ E*

## Exercise 2   (Chapter 4)

| 1 | (i) | GHA | 321°.5748 | | (ii) | GHA | 35°.2158 |
|---|-----|-----|-----------|---|------|-----|----------|
| | | Dec | 22°.2490 S | | | Dec | 16°.0474 S |
| | (ii) | GHA | 22°.4952 | | | | |
| | | Dec | 22°.2715 S | 4 | | GHAγ | 283°.2927 |
| | | | | | | SHA | 146°.2979 |
| 2 | (i) | GHA | 0°.0014 | | | GHA* | 69°.5906 |
| | | Dec | 21°.9791 S | | | Dec | 19°.2821 N |
| | (ii) | GHA | 26°.0292 | 5 | | GHAγ | 91°.9754 |
| | | Dec | 21°.9610 S | | | SHA | 258°.9181 |
| | | | | | | GHA* | 350°.8935 |
| 3 | (i) | GHA | 102°.6848 | | | Dec | 16°.6947 S |
| | | Dec | 21°.6933 N | | | | |

## Exercise 3   (Chapter 5)

| 1 | Lat | −11.1167 | 4 | GMT | 18.6811 |
|---|-----|----------|---|-----|---------|
| | Long | −97.7000 | | Lat | 38.7500 |
| | GHA | 106.2268 | | Long | 3.4500 |
| | LHA | 8.5268 | | GHAγ | 230.5016 |
| | Dec | −9.4247 | | SHA | 112.9286 |
| | Hc | 81.4415 | | GHA* | 343.4302 |
| | Az | 280.6190 | | LHA* | 346.8802 |
| | | | | Dec | −26.3911 |
| 2 | Lat | 51.1833 | | Hc | 23.7126 |
| | Long | 3.0167 | | Az | 167.1687 |
| | GHA | 8.6648 | | | |
| | LHA | 11.6815 | 5 | GMT | 21.0267 |
| | Dec | −22.9474 | | Lat | 45.0000 |
| | Hc | 15.1584 | | Long | −3.2667 |
| | Az | 191.1378 | | GHAγ | 153.4175 |
| | | | | SHA | 80.9214 |
| 3 | Lat | 51.1833 | | GHA* | 234.3389 |
| | Long | 1.9667 | | LHA* | 231.0722 |
| | GHA | 61.6895 | | Dec | 38.7620 |
| | LHA | 63.6562 | | Hc | 5.5240 |
| | Dec | 11.9265 | | Az | 37.5483 |
| | Hc | 25.6691 | | | |
| | Az | 256.6080 | | | |

**Exercise 4**   (Chapter 6)

| 1 | Ho | 81.2500 | 4 | Ho | 24.0167 |
|---|----|---------|---|----|---------|
|   | Hc | 81.2629 |   | Hc | 23.7126 |
|   | p  | −0.0129 |   | p  | 0.3041  |
|   |    |         |   |    |         |
| 2 | Ho | 15.5833 | 5 | Ho | 75.6500 |
|   | Hc | 15.1584 |   | Hc | 75.5240 |
|   | p  | 0.4249  |   | p  | 0.1260  |
|   |    |         |   |    |         |
| 3 | Ho | 39.8500 |   |    |         |
|   | Hc | 39.9365 |   |    |         |
|   | p  | −0.0865 |   |    |         |

**Exercise 5**   (Chapter 7)

1

|          | *Altair* | *Arcturus* |
|----------|----------|------------|
| p        | 0.1543   | 0.0987     |
| Az       | 80.0000  | 335.0000   |

| A | 0.8515 | B | −0.2120 | C | 1.1485 |
|---|--------|---|---------|---|--------|
| D | 0.1162 | E | 0.1102  | G | 0.9330 |

| EP Lat   | −4°.1500  |
|----------|-----------|
| EP Long  | 45°.5167  |
| d.Lat    | 0°.1681   |
| d.Long   | 0°.1274   |
| Fix Lat  | −3°.9819  |
| Fix Long | 45°.6441  |

*Fix     3° 59′ S     45° 39′ E*

2

|    | *Vega*  | *Spica*  | *Dubhe*  |
|----|---------|----------|----------|
| p  | 0.0421  | 0.0096   | −0.0786  |
| Az | 68.0000 | 202.0000 | 325.0000 |

| A | 1.6710  | B | 0.2248 | C | 1.3290 |
|---|---------|---|--------|---|--------|
| D | −0.0575 | E | 0.0805 | G | 2.1702 |

| EP Lat   | 36°.7000  |
|----------|-----------|
| EP Long  | −8°.9167  |
| d.Lat    | −0°.0436  |
| d.Long   | 0°.0848   |
| Fix Lat  | 36°.6564  |
| Fix Long | −8°.8319  |

*Fix     36° 39′ N     8° 50′ W*

3

|         | *Venus*  | *Sun*    |
|---------|----------|----------|
| GMT     | 15.0272  | 15.0514  |
| EP Lat  | 55.8000  | 55.8000  |
| EP Long | −8.9833  | −8.9833  |
| GHA     | 358.7468 | 48.4904  |

| | | |
|---|---|---|
| LHA | 349.7635 | 39.5071 |
| Dec | −24.0723 | −21.8527 |
| Ho | 9.7167 | 5.3167 |
| Hc | 9.6526 | 5.4314 |
| p | 0.0641 | −0.1147 |
| Az | 170.5267 | 216.3790 |

| | | | | | |
|---|---|---|---|---|---|
| A | 1.6211 | B | 0.3152 | C | 0.3789 |
| D | 0.0292 | E | 0.0786 | G | 0.5149 |

| | |
|---|---|
| d.Lat | −0°.0266 |
| d.Long | 0°.4083 |
| Fix Lat | 55°.7734 |
| Fix Long | −8°.5750 |

*Fix     55° 46′ N    8° 34.5′ W*

**4**

| | *Antares* | *Altair* |
|---|---|---|
| GMT | 21.5017 | 21.5372 |
| EP Lat | 35.2833 | 35.2833 |
| EP Long | −18.0333 | −18.0333 |
| A, | 339.0871 | 339.0871 |
| GHAγ | 303.4808 | 304.0156 |
| SHA | 112.9305 | 62.5237 |
| GHA* | 56.4113 | 6.5393 |
| LHA* | 38.3780 | 348.5059 |
| Dec | −26.3911 | 8.8220 |
| Ho | 18.0167 | 61.4500 |
| Hc | 18.4505 | 61.5290 |
| p | −0.4338 | −0.0790 |
| Az | 215.8934 | 155.6032 |

| | | | | | |
|---|---|---|---|---|---|
| A | 1.4857 | B | 0.0988 | C | 0.5143 |
| D | 0.4234 | E | 0.2217 | G | 0.7544 |

| | |
|---|---|
| d.Lat | 0°.2596 |
| d.Long | 0°.4670 |
| Fix Lat | 35°.5429 |
| Fix Long | −17°.5663 |

*Fix     35° 32.5′ N    17° 34′ W*

**5**

| | *Alpheratz* | *Vega* | *Alioth* |
|---|---|---|---|
| GMT | 16.5011 | 16.5333 | 16.5661 |
| EP Lat | 55.5167 | 55.5167 | 55.5167 |
| EP Long | −8.5667 | −8.5667 | −8.5667 |
| A | 68.7810 | 68.7810 | 68.7810 |
| GHAγ | 317.9610 | 318.4456 | 318.9387 |
| SHA | 358.1348 | 80.9235 | 166.6975 |
| GHA* | 316.0958 | 39.3692 | 125.6361 |
| LHA* | 307.5291 | 30.8025 | 117.0695 |
| Dec | 28.9921 | 38.7694 | 56.0564 |

|        | *Alpheratz* | *Vega*    | *Alioth* |
|--------|-------------|-----------|----------|
| Ho     | 44.6500     | 63.2167   | 32.8333  |
| Hc     | 44.5229     | 63.5491   | 32.6808  |
| p      | 0.1271      | −0.3324   | 0.1525   |
| Az     | 103.3638    | 243.6805  | 323.7914 |

| A | 0.9010 | B | −0.3041 | C | 2.0990 |
|---|--------|---|---------|---|--------|
| D | 0.2410 | E | 0.3315  | G | 1.7988 |

| d.Lat    | 0°.3373   |
|----------|-----------|
| d.Long   | 0°.3653   |
| Fix Lat  | 55°.8540  |
| Fix Long | −8°.2014  |

*Fix      55° 51′ N     8° 12′ W*

## Exercise 6   (Chapter 8)

1  EP₁ to EP₂:   d.Lat      −46.9846′

| | | |
|---|---|---|
| | departure | −17.1010 miles |
| | d.Long | −0°.3764 |

|      | EP$_1$    | EP$_2$    |
|------|-----------|-----------|
| Lat  | 41.1667   | 40.3836   |
| Long | 2.5167    | 2.1403    |
| Az   | 120.0000  | 210.0000  |
| p    | 0.2015    | −0.1762   |

| A | 1.0000 | B | 0.0000 | C | 1.0000 |
|---|--------|---|--------|---|--------|
| D | 0.0518 | E | 0.2626 | G | 1.0000 |

| d.Lat    | 0°.0518   |
|----------|-----------|
| d.Long   | 0°.3447   |
| Fix Lat  | 40°.4354  |
| Fix Long | 2.4850    |

*Fix      40° 26′ N     2° 29′ E*

2

|                | d.Lat     | departure  | d.long    |
|----------------|-----------|------------|-----------|
| Start to EP$_1$ | 30.6418′  | −25.7115   | −0°.4285  |
| EP$_1$ to EP$_2$ | 23.6380′  | −8.1392    | −0°.1357  |

|      | EP$_1$    | EP$_2$    |
|------|-----------|-----------|
| Lat  | 0.2440    | 0.6380    |
| Long | −0.2785   | −0.4142   |
| Az   | 100.0000  | 150.0000  |
| p    | −0.1632   | 0.2007    |

| A | 0.7802  | B | −0.6040 | C | 1.2198 |
|---|---------|---|---------|---|--------|
| D | −0.1455 | E | −0.0604 | G | 0.5868 |

| d.Lat   | −0°.3645  |
|---------|-----------|
| d.Long  | −0°.2300  |
| Fix Lat | 0°.2735   |

Fix Long         −0°.6442

*Fix        0° 16′ N    0° 39′ W*

3  EP₁ to EP₂:    d.Lat        10.2606′
                  departure    28.1908 miles
                  d.Long       0°.5810

|         | EP₁       | EP₂      |
|---------|-----------|----------|
| GMT     | 9.2736    | 15.0125  |
| Lat     | 35.9500   | 36.1210  |
| Long    | 1.0833    | 1.6644   |
| GHA     | 321.9135  | 48.0151  |
| LHA     | 322.9969  | 49.6795  |
| Dec     | −4.3763   | −4.4685  |
| Ho      | 37.0167   | 28.0833  |
| Hc      | 36.8563   | 28.3700  |
| p       | 0.1604    | −0.2867  |
| Az      | 131.4100  | 239.7542 |

| A  0.6912 | B  −0.0609 | C  1.3088 |
|-----------|------------|-----------|
| D  0.0383 | E  0.3679  | G  0.9009 |

d.Lat        0°.0805
d.Long       0°.3527
Fix Lat      36°.2015
Fix Long     2°.0171

*Fix        36° 12′ N    2° 01′ E*

4  Venus sight to Altair sight:    d.Lat        17.3205′
                                   departure    −10.0000 miles
                                   d.Long       −0°.2603

|         | *Venus*   | *Altair* |
|---------|-----------|----------|
| GMT     | 15.1803   | 17.5000  |
| Lat     | 50.0333   | 50.3220  |
| Long    | −6.0000   | −6.2603  |
| GHAγ    |           | 357.6265 |
| SHA     |           | 62.5291  |
| GHA     | 12.0409   | 60.1557  |
| LHA     | 6.0409    | 53.8954  |
| Dec     | −17.8442  | 8.8204   |
| Ho      | 21.8333   | 29.5333  |
| Hc      | 21.9127   | 29.3270  |
| p       | −0.0793   | 0.2063   |
| Az      | 186.1987  | 246.3127 |

| A  1.1497  | B  0.4752  | C  0.8503 |
|------------|------------|-----------|
| D  −0.0040 | E  −0.1804 | G  0.7517 |

d.Lat        0°.1095
d.Long       −0°.4281

Fix Lat        50°.4315
Fix Long      −6°.6884

*Fix      50° 26' N   6° 41' W*

5 Moon sight to Star sight:

| | | | |
|---|---|---|---|
| | | d.Lat | −37.0000' |
| | | departure | 64.0859 miles |
| | | d.Long | 1°.2295 |

| | Moon | Regulus |
|---|---|---|
| Date | Oct 1 | Oct 2 |
| GMT | 17.0894 | 6.3625 |
| Lat | 30.0000 | 29.3833 |
| Long | −15.0000 | −13.7705 |
| GHAγ | | 106.3267 |
| SHA | | 208.1545 |
| GHA | 39.6273 | 314.4811 |
| LHA | 24.6273 | ·300.7106 |
| Dec | −12.6689 | 12.0594 |
| Ho | 40.9500 | 32.1500 |
| Hc | 41.1798 | 32.5268 |
| p | −0.2298 | −0.3768 |
| Az | 212.6962 | 94.2850 |

| | | | | | |
|---|---|---|---|---|---|
| A | 0.7138 | B | 0.3801 | C | 1.2862 |
| D | 0.2216 | E | −0.2515 | G | 0.7736 |

d.Lat        0°.4920
d.Long      −0°.3913
Fix Lat      29°.8753
Fix Long    −14°.1618

*Fix      29° 52.5' N   14° 10' W*


**Exercise 7**   (Chapter 9)

1 (a)   50°N      (b)   51°N      (c)   25°S
  (d)   55°S      (e)   12°S      (f)    7°N

2 Ho      −15°.1500
  Dec    −23°.4320
  Lat      51°.4180

*Latitude      51° 25' N*

| 3 | Regulus | Capella |
|---|---|---|
| GMT | 6.7081 | 6.7336 |
| EP Lat | 52.9667 | 52.9667 |
| EP Long | | −5.0167 |
| GHAγ | | 157.2483 |
| SHA | | 281.1575 |
| GHA* | | 78.4058 |

|            | Regulus     | Capella    |
|------------|-------------|------------|
| LHA*       |             | 73.3892    |
| Dec        | 12.0574     | 45.9790    |
| Ho         | −49.0667    | 44.0333    |
| True Lat   | 52.9908     |            |
| Hc         |             | 43.9223    |
| p          | 0.0241      | 0.1110     |
| Az         | 360.0000    | 292.4024   |

| A  1.1452 | B  −0.3523 | C  0.8548 |
|-----------|------------|-----------|
| D  0.0664 | E  −0.1026 | G  0.8548 |

d.Long    −0°.1828
Fix Long  −5°.1995

*Fix    52° 59.5′ N    5° 12′ W*

4 Sun sight to Moon sight:
|          |                  |
|----------|------------------|
| d.Lat    | −25.7115′        |
| departure| −30.6418 miles   |
| d.Long   | −0°.8348         |

|          | Sun       | Moon      |
|----------|-----------|-----------|
| GMT      | 8.0386    | 18.0692   |
| EP Lat   | 52.5000   | 52.0715   |
| EP Long  | 4.0667    | 3.2318    |
| GHA      | 303.5347  |           |
| LHA      | 307.6014  |           |
| Dec      | −5.1262   | −21.3043  |
| Ho       | 17.6000   | −16.6333  |
| True Lat |           | 52.0624   |
| Hc       | 17.4019   |           |
| p        | 0.1981    | −0.0091   |
| Az       | 124.2127  | 360.0000  |

| A   1.3161 | B  −0.4650 | C  0.6839 |
|------------|------------|-----------|
| D  −0.1205 | E   0.1638 | G  0.6839 |

d.Long    0°.3796
Fix Long  3°.6114

*Fix    52° 04′ N    3° 37′ E*

5 Venus sight to Vega sight:
|         |               |
|---------|---------------|
| d.Lat   | 7.5000′       |
| dep     | 12.9904 miles |
| d.Long  | 0°.3481       |

|         | Venus     | Vega      |
|---------|-----------|-----------|
| GMT     | 14.6014   | 17.0000   |
| EP Lat  | 51.4833   | 51.6083   |
| EP Long | 0.7667    | 1.1148    |
| GHAγ    |           | 344.1921  |
| SHA     |           | 80.9237   |
| GHA*    |           | 65.1158   |

| LHA* | | 66.2306 |
|---|---|---|
| Dec | −19.3904 | 38.7678 |
| Ho | −19.1333 | 43.3667 |
| True Lat | 51.4763 | |
| Hc | | 43.3099 |
| p | −0.0070 | 0.0568 |
| Az | 360.0000 | 281.2983 |

| A | 1.0384 | B | −0.1921 | C | 0.9616 |
|---|---|---|---|---|---|
| D | 0.0041 | E | −0.0557 | G | 0.9616 |

| d.Lat | −0°.0070 |
|---|---|
| d.Long | −0°.0955 |
| Fix Lat | 51°.6013 |
| Fix long | 1°.0193 |

*Fix   51° 36′ N   1° 01′ E*

**Exercise 8**   (Chapter 10)

| 1 | SHA | 326.8494 |
|---|---|---|
| | p | 0.8269 |

| 2 | GHAγ | 23.2645 |
|---|---|---|
| | GHA* | 350.1139 |
| | EP Long | −92.0000 |
| | LHA* | 258.1139 |
| | C | −0.1703 |
| | S | −0.8092 |
| | Ho | 59.5000 |
| | True Lat | 59.6800 |
| | EP Lat | 60.0000 |
| | Intercept p | −0.3200 |
| | Az | 1.5943 |

*Latitude   59° 41′ N     Azimuth   1°.5943     Intercept   −0°.3200*

| 3 | GHAγ | 165.0607 |
|---|---|---|
| | SHA | 326.9812 |
| | GHA* | 132.0419 |
| | EP Long | 6.0000 |
| | LHA* | 138.0419 |
| | p | 0.8260 |
| | C | −0.6142 |
| | S | 0.5522 |
| | Ho | 39.7833 |
| | True Lat | 40.3998 |
| | EP Lat | 40.0000 |
| | Intercept p | 0.3998 |
| | Az | 359.2814 |

*Latitude   40° 24′ N     Azimuth   359°.2814     Intercept   0°.3998*

| 4 | *Polaris* | *Regulus* |
|---|---|---|
| GMT | 19.5000 | 19.5500 |
| EP Lat | 30.9500 | 30.9500 |
| EP Long | −18.6667 | −18.6667 |
| GHAγ | 125.5265 | 126.2786 |
| SHA | 327.0854 | 208.1531 |
| polar distance | 0.8213 | |
| GHA* | 92.6119 | 334.4317 |
| LHA* | 73.9452 | 315.7650 |
| C | 0.2271 | |
| S | 0.7893 | |
| Dec | | 12.0586 |
| Ho | 31.4167 | 45.1333 |
| Hc | | 45.1009 |
| True Lat | 31.1928 | |
| p | 0.2428 | 0.0324 |
| Az | 359.0752 | 104.8734 |

| A | 1.0656 | B | −0.2642 | C | 0.9344 |
|---|---|---|---|---|---|
| D | 0.2345 | E | 0.0274 | G | 0.9259 |

| d.Lat | 0°.2445 |
|---|---|
| d.Long | 0°.1148 |
| Fix Lat | 31°.1945 |
| Fix Long | −18.5519 |

*Fix      31° 12′ N      18° 33′ W*

5 Polaris sight to Sun sight:

| | d.Lat | 21.6506′ |
|---|---|---|
| | departure | 12.5000 miles |
| | d.Long | 0°.3009 |

| | *Polaris* | *Sun* |
|---|---|---|
| GMT | 6.0467 | 10.5367 |
| EP Lat | 46.0000 | 46.3608 |
| Ep Long | −5.0000 | −4.6991 |
| GHAγ | 135.0882 | |
| SHA | 326.2737 | |
| polar distance | 0.8190 | |
| GHA | 101.3618 | 342.1424 |
| LHA | 96.3618 | 337.4433 |
| C | −0.0907 | |
| S | 0.8139 | |
| Dec | | −15.7193 |
| Ho | 45.8667 | 24.8000 |
| Hc | | 24.6717 |
| True Lat | 45.9634 | |
| p | −0.0366 | 0.1283 |
| Az | 358.8311 | 156.0245 |

| A | 1.8345 | B | −0.3917 | C | 0.1655 |
|---|---|---|---|---|---|
| D | −0.1538 | E | 0.0529 | G | 0.1502 |

| | |
|---|---|
| d.Lat | −0°.0316 |
| d.Long | 0°.3544 |
| Fix Lat | 46°.3292 |
| Fix Long | −4°.3447 |

*Fix    46° 20′N    4° 21′W*

## Exercise 9  (Chapter 11)

1 (a) 1242    (b) 1442    (c) 11h08m12s    (d) 20h25m12s
2 (a) 1306    (b) 1106    (c) 1906
3 (a) 2019    (b) 1019    (c) 2319
4 (a) 1717 May 23    (b)2217 May 23    (c) 0617 May 24
5 (a)  0906 GMT GD October 15
  (b)  21h56m52s GMT GD October 14

## Exercise 10  (Chapter 12)

1
| d.Lat | −37.0000′ |
|---|---|
| d.Long | 1°.9000 |
| departure | 70.7459 miles |
| course | 117°.6095 |
| distance | 79.8372 |

*Course    118°    Distance    80 miles*

2
| d.Lat | 1377.0000′ |
|---|---|
| d.Long | 1987.0000′ |
| M Pts Mombassa | −240.5632 |
| M Pts Bombay | 1148.6557 |
| DMP | 1389.2190 |
| course | 55°.0405 |
| distance | 2403.1543 |

*Course    055°    Distance    2403 miles*

3
| d.Long | 35°.8167 |
|---|---|
| d | 51°.1219 |
| 60d | 3067.3146 |
| course | 139°.8921 |

*Distance    3067 miles    Initial Course 140°*

4
| d.Long | −62°.3833 |
|---|---|
| d | 55°.7463 |
| 60d | 3344.7799 |
| course | 299°.5401 |

*Distance    3345 miles    Initial Course    300°*

| 5 | d.Long | −43°.7500 |
|---|---|---|
| | d | 56°.4376 |
| | 60d | 3386.2550 |
| | d.Lat | −2620.0000′ |
| | d.Long | −2625.0000′ |
| | M Pts Ascension | −478.3285 |
| | M Pts Port Stanley | −3614.5734 |
| | DMP | −3136.2449 |
| | distance | 3416.6139 |

*Great Circle   3386 miles        Rhumb Line   3417 miles*

### Exercise 11 (Chapter 13)

| 1 | Dec | 44.3246 |
|---|---|---|
| | GHA$\gamma$ | 240.6991 |
| | LHA$\gamma$ | 275.6991 |
| | LHA* | 34.6334 |
| | SHA | 49.6675 |

*Star:   Deneb*

| 2 | | Venus | Mars | Jupiter | Saturn |
|---|---|---|---|---|---|
| | GMT | 5.5000 | 5.5000 | 5.5000 | 5.5000 |
| | Lat | 51.3000 | 51.3000 | 51.3000 | 51.3000 |
| | Long | 1.6667 | 1.6667 | 1.6667 | 1.6667 |
| | GHA | 224.3039 | 310.9946 | 254.6118 | 259.3842 |
| | LHA | 225.9706 | 312.6613 | 256.2785 | 261.0509 |
| | Dec | −19.4145 | 16.7642 | −5.9485 | −2.7472 |
| | Hc | −42.0104 | 39.1090 | −13.2023 | −7.7329 |
| | Az | | 114.8470 | | |

*Planet:   Mars*

| 3 | | Star 1 | Star 2 |
|---|---|---|---|
| | EP Lat | 28.0000 | 28.0000 |
| | EP Long | −88.0000 | −88.0000 |
| | LT | 19.0000 | 19.0500 |
| | GMT | 0.8667 | 0.9167 |
| | GD | 25 | 25 |
| | Ho | 22.1667 | 33.2000 |
| | Az | 92.0000 | 160.0000 |
| | Dec | 8.5456 | −25.9252 |
| | A | 277.9770 | 277.9770 |
| | GHA$\gamma$ | 315.6543 | 316.4063 |
| | LHA$\gamma$ | 227.6543 | 228.4063 |
| | LHA* | 69.3767 | 18.5549 |
| | SHA | 62.9690 | 113.0388 |

| Star | Altair | Antares |
|---|---|---|
| SHA | 62.5234 | 112.9284 |
| LHA* | 290.1777 | 341.3347 |
| Dec | 8.8207 | −26.3912 |
| Hc | 21.8974 | 32.7278 |
| p | 0.2693 | 0.4722 |
| Az | 91.5210 | 160.0753 |

| A | 0.8846 | B | −0.3469 | C | 1.1154 |
|---|---|---|---|---|---|
| D | −0.4511 | E | 0.4301 | G | 0.8663 |

| | |
|---|---|
| d.Lat | −0°.4085 |
| d.Long | 0°.2928 |
| Fix Lat | 27°.5915 |
| Fix long | −87°.7072 |

*Fix    27° 35.5′N   87° 42.5′W*

4 Star Sight    Dec      12.9491
                GHAγ    217.2470
                LHA*     62.3865
                SHA     209.9728

*Star:   Regulus*

| Planet Sight | Venus | Mars | Jupiter | Saturn |
|---|---|---|---|---|
| GMT | 8.1406 | 8.1406 | 8.1406 | 8.1406 |
| EP Lat | 53.7000 | 53.7000 | 53.7000 | 53.7000 |
| EP Long | −4.8333 | −4.8333 | −4.8333 | −4.8333 |
| GHA | 267.0453 | 32.2460 | 4.3551 | 17.3482 |
| LHA | 262.2120 | 27.4127 | 359.5218 | 12.5149 |
| Dec | −17.6690 | 0.0584 | −12.2161 | −6.0336 |
| Hc | −18.7266 | 31.7598 | 24.0826 | 29.3427 |
| Az | | 212.7841 | 179.4881 | 194.3124 |

| | Regulus | Jupiter |
|---|---|---|
| GMT | 8.1014 | 8.1406 |
| SHA | 208.1441 | |
| GHA* | 65.3911 | |
| LHA* | 60.5578 | |
| Dec | 12.0554 | −12.2161 |
| Ho | 26.6167 | −24.2500 |
| True Lat | | 53.5339 |
| Hc | 26.9304 | |
| p | −0.3137 | −0.1661 |
| Az | 252.7915 | 360.000 |

| A | 1.0875 | B | 0.2826 | C | 0.9125 |
|---|---|---|---|---|---|
| D | −0.0733 | E | 0.2997 | G | 0.9125 |

| | |
|---|---|
| d.Long | 0°.6416 |
| Fix long | −4°.1917 |

*Fix    53° 32′N   4° 11.5′W*

5 Star Sight    Dec     &minus;16.1506
                GHAγ   91.7403
                LHAγ  106.1070
                LHA*    8.0611
                SHA   261.9542

*Star:  Sirius*

Sirius sight to Moon sight:    d.Lat        0.3486'
                                  departure  &minus;3.9848 miles
                                  d.Long    &minus;0°.0802

|        | *Sirius*  | *Moon*   |
|--------|-----------|----------|
| GMT    | 4.5408    | 5.0467   |
| EP Lat | 34.1333   | 34.1391  |
| EP Long| 14.3667   | 14.2864  |
| SHA    | 258.9124  |          |
| GHA    | 350.6527  | 55.1458  |
| LHA    | 5.0194    | 69.4322  |
| Dec    | −16.6884  | 11.8384  |
| Ho     | 39.1333   | 23.2000  |
| Hc     | 38.9539   | 23.5608  |
| p      | 0.1794    | −0.3608  |
| Az     | 186.1868  | 268.5518 |

A   0.9890    B   0.1324    C   1.0110
D  &minus;0.1692    E   0.3414    G   0.9823

d.Lat             &minus;0°.2202
d.Long           0°.4428
Fix Lat         33°.9190
Fix Long      14°.7292

*Fix    33° 55' N   14° 44' E*


**Exercise 12**   (Chapter 14)

1 *Apparent altitude 23°.9878*

2 H     37.6843
   R     0.0210
   Ho   37.6633

   *True altitude   37° 39'.8*

3 H     30.2282
   R     0.0278
   HP   0.0020
   Ho   30.2022

   *True altitude   30° 12'.1*

4 H     58.5659
   R     0.0099
   HP   0.9671
   Ho   58.7961

   *True altitude   58° 47'.8*

5 H     42.0277
   R     0.0180
   S     0.2650
   Ho   42.2765

   *True altitude   42° 16'.6*

# Index